PRAISE FOR
20 WOMEN STORYTELLERS

"Read along and hear these 20 women roar. They are passionate about words and images and people. It's not unusual for them to take great risks documenting life with raw honesty. **These storytellers lead by listening and watching before they capture the story in print or with their cameras or both.** They enhance our understanding of the world with their superb vision."

—**Bonnie Strauss**, Award-winning Television Correspondent and Documentary Filmmaker

"*20 Women Storytellers* is one-stop shopping for women spotlighting the truth while sharing their talent of the journalist's pen, the photographer's eye or the documentarian's lens. **These truly life-changing women use their words and pictures to inspire, to connect, and to improve our world.** If you have a story to tell, look no further than their examples, which have given a voice to the voiceless, and, in the process, have made a difference."

—**Samantha Harris**, Emmy-winning TV Host, Certified Health Coach, Author of *Your Healthiest Healthy*

"Women telling other women's stories is a long, wonderful tradition that continues in this excellent book of interviews with 20 outstanding documentary filmmakers, journalists, photojournalists and historians. These professionals' work is not limited to women's stories, of course. But in my view, **it is no accident that so many of the stories here—of women and men and children—likely would not have been told without these media-makers' interest and bravery in telling them.**"

> —**Jane Hall**, Associate Professor, School of Communication at American University, Washington, D.C.

"Whether we tell them to ourselves or others, stories give life meaning. They engage people in a way that unadorned information does not. If you are passionate about leading, teaching, selling, entertaining, reporting or causing change, storytelling can give you power. **A fascinating look at the challenges and triumphs of telling stories from the inspiring, diverse role models who are featured here.**"

> —**Paula Gianturco**, Award-winning Photographer and Author

"Following up on *20 Women Changemakers*, editors Pamela Burke and Patricia Caso offer up earnest and creative interviews with *20 Women Storytellers*, changemakers in their own right. Collectively, they represent the wide range of women who impact us through their journalism, creative endeavors, and other story-telling projects around the world. **An accessible, important, and timely contribution.**"

> —**Pamela Stewart**, Ph.D., Historian
> Arizona State University

The Women's Eye Spotlights

20 WOMEN
STORYTELLERS

TAKING ACTION WITH POWERFUL
WORDS AND IMAGES

Cover photos left to right:
Top row: Heidi Levine, Karen Shell, Mimo Khair, Dionne Searcey, Elaine Weiss
Row two: Fernanda Santos, Stacey Reiss, Zahra Hankir, Eleanor Clift, Kim Covington
Row three: Lee Woodruff, Jessica Yu, Lindsey Seavert, Sarah Burns, Carlotta Gall
Row four: Laura Munson, Betsy West, Julie Cohen, Clarissa Ward, Laurie Burrows Grad

The Women's Eye Spotlights

20 WOMEN STORYTELLERS

TAKING ACTION WITH POWERFUL WORDS AND IMAGES

EDITED BY PAMELA BURKE
AND PATRICIA CASO

THE WOMEN'S EYE

Copyright © 2021 by The Women's Eye

All rights reserved. No part of this publication may be reproduced, distributed, or transmitted in any form or by any means, including photocopying, recording, or other electronic or mechanical methods, without the prior written permission of the publisher, except in the case of brief quotations embodied in critical reviews and certain other noncommercial uses permitted by copyright law.

For media and permission requests, contact the publisher at the website below.

www.thewomenseye.com

ISBN: 978-1-7359954-1-0 (print)
ISBN: 978-1-7359954-0-3 (eBook)

Edited by:
Pamela Burke and Patricia Caso
Cover and interior design by Jim Shubin—BookAlchemist.net

Publisher's Cataloging-in-Publication data

Names: Burke, Pamela, editor. | Caso, Patricia, editor.
Title: The Women's Eye spotlights 20 women storytellers : taking action with powerful words and images / edited by Pamela Burke and Patricia Caso.
Series: The Women's Eye Spotlights
Description: Phoenix, AZ: The Women's Eye, 2021.
Identifiers: LCCN: xxxxxxxxx | ISBN 978-1-7359954-1-0 (pbk.) | 978-1-7359954-0-3 (eBook)
Subjects: LCSH Women--Biography. | Women--Biography--Pictorial works. | Social reformers--Biography. | Journalists--Biography. | BISAC BIOGRAPHY & AUTOBIOGRAPHY / Women | BIOGRAPHY & AUTOBIOGRAPHY / Editors, Journalists, Publishers | PHOTOGRAPHY / Photoessays & Documentaries
Classification: LCC PN471 W66 2021 | DDC 810.9/9287/0904--dc23

To the women who have shared their stories with The Women's Eye openly and from their hearts, inspiring future storytellers.

Contents

Acknowledgments		xv
Introduction		xx
Part I: Documentarians—Recording Their Stories		
1.	Directors **Betsy West** and **Julie Cohen** on Their Groundbreaking Movie *RBG*	1
2.	Award-Winning Director **Jessica Yu** Spotlights Heroic Journalist Gladys Kalibbala's Passion	13
3.	Reporter **Lindsey Seavert** Documents the Transformation of a Failing School in the Award-Winning *Love Them First*	25
4.	**Sarah Burns** on Filmmaking, Criminal Injustice and the Central Park Five	37
5.	*Spaceship Earth* Producer **Stacey Reiss** on Biosphere 2 and How Small Groups Can Make Big Change	47

Part II: Photographers—Filming Their Subjects

6. Combat Photojournalist **Heidi Levine** on Covering Deadly War Zones — 61

7. Photographer **Karen Shell** on Keeping Kids in Focus with a Camera Lens — 71

8. Global Photographer **Mimo Khair** Captures the Common Thread of Humanity — 83

Part III: Journalists—Reporting on Their Worlds

9. Pulitzer Prize-Winning War Journalist **Carlotta Gall** on Getting the Story Right — 97

10. New York Times Journalist **Dionne Searcey** on Her Pursuit of Disobedient Women in West Africa — 109

11. *The Woman's Hour* Author **Elaine Weiss** on the Dramatic Battle for the Right to Vote — 121

12. Journalist **Fernanda Santos** on Covering One of the Deadliest Days in American Firefighting from the Human Angle — 133

13. Debut Author **Zahra Hankir** Spotlights Arab Women Reporters in Their Own Words — 145

Part IV: Broadcasters—Using Their Voices

14. International Correspondent **Clarissa Ward** Witnesses History *On All Fronts* — 159

15. **Eleanor Clift** on Gabrielle Giffords and the Washington She Knows — 171

16. Broadcaster-Turned-Activist **Kim Covington:** From Finding Golden Nuggets to Serving the Community — 183

17. **Lee Woodruff** on Family, Creating a Foundation and Reinvention — 195

Part V: Impacters—Inspiring Their Readers

18. Writing Retreat Leader **Laura Munson** on Women at Their "Now What?" Crossroads — 207

19. Blogger **Laurie Burrows Grad** on Grief, Widowhood and Recovering from Tragic Loss — 219

In Memory

20.	Broadcaster **Cokie Roberts** Celebrates the Triumphs of Our Courageous Founding Mothers	233

Advice from our Storytellers	243
Book Club Discussion Questions	251
Websites for Storyteller Updates	252
Photo Permissions	255
Books from our Storytellers	257
About the Podcast Hosts—Stacey Gualandi and Catherine Anaya	259
About the Editors—Pamela Burke and Patricia Caso	261

Acknowledgments

What an honor to work with the people who have joined me to put together *20 Women Storytellers*. We have a strong team who cares deeply about all forms of journalism, the truth, and making a difference.

My co-editor Patricia Caso is an integral part of this process as she was in assembling our first book, *20 Women Changemakers: Taking Action Around the World*. She has worked tirelessly to contact people, track down photographs and information and spend time with our interviewees to tell their stories in the best possible way.

Our fearless radio and podcast hosts Stacey Gualandi and Catherine Anaya have contributed a wealth of ideas and memorable interviews with the accomplished storytellers in this anthology. We thank these award-winning journalists for the endless energy and enthusiasm they bring to their work.

Some of their interviews were recorded for *The Women's Eye Radio Show* in Phoenix, Arizona. We thank Jonathan Molina and his crew for their assistance in producing our program at 1480 KPHX.

Podcasting has been an exciting new way to tell our TWE stories. We want to thank Catherine Scrivano, founder of CASCO Financial Group, for her constant support and contribution to our podcasts and website.

Kudos go to Garrett Miller, our expert on all things related to the internet, podcasts and website, for his dedication to *The Women's Eye*. He has been our webmaster; his ability to deal with all technical questions at the drop of a hat amazes us. We also salute his prowess at posting our podcasts and expertise with social media.

Hats off to all the people involved in taping our podcasts both in Las Vegas, Nevada, for Stacey and in Phoenix, Arizona, for Catherine. Matt Smith and Jesus Rodriguez at Adrenaline Studios were a tremendous help to organize our efforts and record interviews in Nevada.

Phoenix's CO+HOOTS Coworking Space was our headquarters for many of Catherine's recordings. We can't thank its founder Jenny Poon and all of her staff enough for their professionalism and assistance.

ACKNOWLEDGMENTS

Our website adviser Cheryl McLaughlin continues to assist us with many facets of the website, designing and maintaining it with the constant demands of modern technology. We appreciate her professional approach to the presentation of our interviews and stories.

We continue to have a great love of books and thank the folks at independent bookstores, particularly Changing Hands in Phoenix and Book Passage in Corte Madera, California for making us aware of new books and live author events.

We are grateful to all the book publicists, agents, and public relations representatives who introduce us to amazing storytellers.

We thank Laurie McAndish King and Jim Shubin, the publishing team who oversaw the production of *20 Women Changemakers* as well as this book. We can always count on their expert attention to detail and design and appreciate their contribution. Their advice is invaluable.

Our gratitude goes out to the women who have let us into their lives and given us their time so we can share their stories. Their dedication to listening to others, to understanding the world, and passion to find solutions to problems is life-affirming. Some feel they can be a voice for people who don't have one; others want to change the world. They all want to tell stories that connect us. And for this we appreciate and thank them!

—Pamela Burke

"It has been said that next to hunger and thirst, our most basic human need is for storytelling."

—Khalil Gibran, Writer and Poet

Introduction

As a follow-up to our *20 Women Changemakers* book, we want to share our interviews with a wide range of fascinating documentarians, photographers, journalists, broadcasters and impacters.

In this book we spotlight *20 Women Storytellers* who inspire and motivate us. They are each driven by their passion to make a difference with their words and photographs. What is most exciting about these storytellers is that they come in all forms; we think you will enjoy their unique stories.

We interviewed documentarians who find a person or a project they are so passionate about, they simply can't stop until they make a film.

— When documentarians **Betsy West** and **Julie Cohen** met the "rockstar" octogenarian Supreme Court Justice Ruth Bader Ginsberg and learned how she had worked to create equality for the genders, they knew they had to tell the story of her personal and professional life.

— When director **Jessica Yu** discovered that Ugandan journalist Gladys Kalibbala was rescuing hundreds of lost and abandoned children on her own, she knew she wanted to feature Gladys in a documentary and bring her story to life in a book.

— When television reporter **Lindsey Seavert** met school principal Mauri Melander Friestleben and saw her unflinching strength and love for students at a neglected elementary school, she was determined to discover how Mauri and the teachers were saving those children from failure.

— When filmmaker **Sarah Burns** was researching a book about the headline-grabbing story of the Central Park jogger, she couldn't rest until she unearthed the truth about the five teens known as The Central Park Five, who were falsely accused of what had been called "the crime of the century." It became Sarah's first documentary.

— When film producer **Stacey Reiss** heard about eight environmentalists quarantining themselves inside a giant replica of the Earth's ecosystem, she knew she wanted to make a movie about the way a small team made a big environmental difference by living in Biosphere 2.

Storytelling has always been a powerful tool to help us remember events, record history and uncover truths.

Not only has the way we tell stories evolved dramatically over the ages, but so has the approach, as these women demonstrate.

Some of our interviewees chose the camera as a vehicle to show the world how photographic images can connect people and change lives.

— Combat photographer **Heidi Levine** dodges bullets in some of the world's most dangerous war zones to tell human stories, because she's always wanted to use the power of photography to help others.

— Professional photographer **Karen Shell** found a way to use the camera to heal children living with trauma through her life-changing non-profit, Kids in Focus.

— Global photographer **Mimo Khair** wants to show the positive side of humanity and strives to create art that can "do something."

Our journalists may not use the camera, but they use all available writing instruments on their mission to get the story and get it right. Finding the truth is important to them. We found their dedication to be remarkable.

— *New York Times* reporters **Carlotta Gall** and **Dionne Searcey** found their stories in the war zones of Afghanistan, Pakistan, and West Africa. They were awarded Pulitzer Prizes for their outstanding work.

— **Zahra Hankir** is passionate for people to understand the Arab world. She searched out 19 courageous reporters who tell their stories about surviving conflict and violence in their Middle Eastern homelands.

— Writers in America are searching for their truth in newsmaking stories of the past and present. Journalist-author **Elaine Weiss** spent five years chronicling the six-week battle leading up to the historic day women won the right to vote in 1920.

— Journalist **Fernanda Santos** tells stories from the human angle. Her drive to understand the world led her to write a book about the 19 firefighters who perished in Arizona's deadly Yarnell Fire—told with a very personal approach.

Our storytellers make their impact in many ways; several have done it on camera. As broadcasters, they have told their stories on video as well as in print.

— We salute **Eleanor Clift**, who has reported on Washington goings-on for over five decades.

Known for her honesty, she says, "It's a lot easier to be honest than to figure out tortured ways of covering up what the truth is."

— International correspondent **Clarissa Ward** felt a calling to humanize people in her reports from some of the world's most dangerous regions because, as she says, "Their stories need to be told somewhere."

— **Lee Woodruff** and **Kim Covington** have always had a passion for telling stories and finding solutions. Their hearts have also been in the nonprofit world where they help people on the other side of the camera deal with issues affecting refugees, veterans and people in need.

Technology allows us to tell our stories in endless ways now. Who would ever have thought we'd advance from scratches on the wall of a cave to a blog on the internet or a story on Instagram? The evolution astounds me, as I started my own storytelling on a hectograph or gelatin tray. I was obsessed with telling stories about my neighborhood as a second grader, going from house to house interviewing people about their exciting summer plans and projects.

I would take their stories, type them up on a special paper, and put that paper face down on the gelatin to make a master. After a brief waiting period, the gelatin could be used as a copy machine. A neighborhood newspaper was born, duplicated and circulated.

It's from those primitive roots that I marvel at the storytellers of our age—the bloggers, podcasters, and social media mavens who want to spread their word in all forms available.

— Writer **Laurie Burrows Grad** found blogging to be the best way to deal with the grief of her husband's passing and to spread her story to others in hope that her experiences would be of help.

— From her home in Montana, bestselling author **Laura Munson** gathers friends from near and far to her writing retreats, where they can share their stories as they build new "bridge" communities.

— To cap off our storyteller interviews, we are honored to end our book with pioneer journalist and legendary broadcaster **Cokie Roberts**, who passed away in 2019. She had a unique love of history, particularly that of our Founding Mothers.

Cokie gave us a new understanding of their resilience and patriotism through the stories she uncovered. We treasure the time she spent with us sharing her journalistic observations and experiences.

Whether it's by camera, book, computer or as it was by hectograph, the stories that are the most memorable, as Fernanda Santos says, are "those that get people to care and want to change things." Perhaps these interviews will inspire you to share your ideas and tell your stories.

—Pamela Burke

Part I
DOCUMENTARIANS: RECORDING THEIR STORIES

"It's incredible to see the creativity, beauty and hardships people capture when filmmaking is opened up and shared with the world."

—*Jehane Noujaim*, Photographer, Journalist and Documentarian

Betsy West and Julie Cohen

Directors Betsy West and Julie Cohen on Their Groundbreaking Movie *RBG*

By Stacey Gualandi

I am very fortunate to be able to speak with two of the most talked-about, award-winning documentary filmmakers right now, Julie Cohen and Betsy West, the directors of *RBG*.

> "This was the first really massive project we took on together as partners. It was an exciting, big and ambitious partnership which really paid off beautifully."
> —*Betsy West*

In 2015, they joined forces with a brilliant idea—let's make a film about Ruth Bader Ginsburg, a champion of gender equality who ultimately became a United States Supreme Court justice and a pop culture icon, aka the Notorious RBG.

As successful journalists, professors and producers, Julie and Betsy are trailblazers in their own right...

EYE: I'm talking to you after opening weekend. Are you in the glow of that right now? How are you ladies feeling?

BETSY: It was very exciting to be at the theater and see the response. Many theaters were sold out.

> **We understand that it did very well and we're very excited for people to see this film that we've been working on for so long. It's so great to launch it out into the world and have people respond this way.**

JULIE: It was really fun seeing people show up: grown women and their Notorious RBG T-shirts, sometimes children coming in little Justice Ginsburg robes and collars. There's a high level of enthusiasm for the subject matter and the movie.

EYE: What I love about this project, too, as I look at the credits, it's Betsy, Julie, Carla, Claudia, Amy, Courtney, Alexandra; it's all women. Was that a conscious decision to all collectively come together to talk about this really wonderful woman, Ruth Bader Ginsburg?

BETSY: Absolutely. We figured we're doing a story about one of the most important women in our country who has been such a trailblazer for women and why not hire, first of all, a female Director of Photography.

So we got the wonderful Claudia and then it went on from there. We worked with a few men and that worked out all right.

EYE: But when tackling a subject or a person of this caliber, I think it needs a woman's touch perhaps in telling her story. You both had interviewed the Justice at different times, in your news careers. What was it about her that made you think this woman was worthy of a documentary, and of everybody knowing what she has accomplished?

JULIE: It was really a combination of two things. On the one hand, you've got the current-day excitement over RBG, who is an unlikely pop culture phenomenon. This tiny little intellectual octogenarian grandmother became a rock star to people who appreciated her two cents and loved that she was speaking truth to power.

> **Also, she basically charted a course to create equality for the genders under the law in the US Constitution. She brought a series of cases, six cases to the Supreme Court. She won five of them.**

That helped ensure that women and men were going to be treated equally under the law. That's a pretty huge story and it's just not widely known enough in our view.

EYE: Thanks for bringing this to our attention! In a recent interview you said that what this does is show just how important the Supreme Court is and how much it matters to our lives. Right?

BETSY: Yes. I think a lot of people don't remember that not so long ago women were second-class citizens. A woman could be fired for getting pregnant, and if she wanted to get a credit card she had to get the permission of her husband. And husbands were never prosecuted for raping their wives. When RBG got through with her work at the Supreme Court, that had all changed.

> **We thought it was really important for people to see how she effected that change. And what we owe her.**

EYE: Exactly. So Julie, why do you think *RBG* is the right film about the right woman at the right time? Because a lot's happened just in the three years since you both decided to do this documentary.

JULIE: When we were starting this project in early 2015, one question was, *Is she having a cultural moment right now? Is this project too late?* But that was that not an issue.

In the three years since, she's just become more relevant. She was already very much seen as an important cultural figure for liberals due to some of the very strong defense arguments she presented in response to some of the opinions written by the court's conservative majority.

Add to that the current cultural relevance related to the Time's Up and Me Too movements, the idea of women now speaking up for the rights they still haven't gained in the workplace.

EYE: You both have built amazing careers. Do you credit her for paving the way for both of your successes and for actually making this movie?

BETSY: I began my career in the 1970s. I'm really a result of the women's movement, which opened up opportunities for me and many other women who are able to go into professions that were not open to women even ten years earlier.

I was not aware of what Ruth Bader Ginsburg was doing in the Supreme Court to broaden not just opportunities but *rights* for women in America. I don't think that it was all that well known.

> **People were marching in the streets and fighting for equality. And there she was in this Supreme Court chamber arguing on behalf of women to really expand our legal rights.**

EYE: She has the most amazing work ethic; I think that was very surprising.

JULIE: When someone's as successful as Ruth Bader Ginsburg, it's probably not surprising that she works hard, but just *how* hard she worked and the extent to which, even in her later years, she's staying up until two or three in the morning.

When she's not working, she's at the opera. That was a bit surprising, not to mention her great sense of humor. She's known as a reserved and serious person, but she has a belly laugh that's better than just about anybody's I've heard.

EYE: That's fantastic! What was also amazing in this film, keeping your journalism background front and center, was how you found the actual, real-life people at the center of many of these cases that she brought to the Supreme Court, people like Sharron Frontiero, Stephen Wiesenfeld and Lilly Ledbetter, whom we have interviewed on our radio program.

> **There were real people involved in this who were directly affected, and the legal results ultimately affected everyone in this country.**

BETSY: We were so lucky to be able to talk to all three of those people. Ruth Bader Ginsburg, the lawyer, initially was arguing on behalf of real people. She saw discrimination that was affecting human beings and she found the most sympathetic cases to bring before nine male justices to make them understand why these laws were wrong, and were just unfair.

You hear Sharron Frontiero talk about her story as a young married Air Force lieutenant who discovers one day that her male counterparts are getting a housing allowance that she doesn't get. Then she goes to ask about it and is told in a very matter of fact way, *No, no, no, you're a woman.*

> **And then she thinks this is a mistake, and realizes that she's going to have to bring a lawsuit. She found the right lawyer to represent her, Ruth Bader Ginsburg, who took that case and won it for her.**

EYE: One of the lines from the film is from Justice Ginsburg when she says, "Enduring real change happens one step at a time." What I'm wondering is, have we come a long way baby, or do we still have a lot of work to do?

JULIE: I think both. I think you're right to focus on the strategic side of Ruth Bader Ginsburg, her very deliberately taking one step at a time, a step-by-step approach to the change she wanted to make and she wanted to see in the world—part of that was taking on a man to represent.

One of the early cases she accepted was Stephen Wiesenfeld, a young widower. His wife died in childbirth. He wanted to raise his young son at home and went to the Social Security office hoping to get the benefits that a widow would get and was told no, those benefits are only for a woman whose husband dies, not vice versa. That seemed unfair to him.

She argued it before the Supreme Court, knowing she was talking to nine male justices. What better way to get them to see that when we don't treat the genders equally—and maybe that's really not so good or so fair— than to bring in this really sympathetic young father who could have been one of them?

EYE: It's amazing how you were able to make this an entertaining film, a love story between Justice Ginsburg and her husband Marty. There were so many aspects to it but it's also very educational.

BETSY: I think that the challenge of telling, as you say, an important story and telling the heart of it are these great cases and figuring out a way to tell them for people who are not lawyers. I'm not a lawyer and that's always a challenge to me.

The other thing is that Justice Ginsburg has had a very long and eventful life. It was a challenge to go back and forth between her personal life, to explore who she is and the things she accomplished.

EYE: There's no doubt that her legal legacy is going to live on. Is there something about this film, in addition to letting everyone know that the Supreme Court really matters to our lives, that you really want people to grasp?

JULIE: We wanted people to get to know the Justice as a human being. We wanted them to understand the impact that she's had on the law that people might not have known about.

But we also wanted to show how someone's personal life can interplay with their professional life, especially for a woman.

Justice Ginsburg made the point that one of the most important career moves she made in her life, quite early, was choosing to fall in love with and marry fellow undergraduate at Cornell University, Marty Ginsburg.

She was, as you'll see from the home movies in our film, an extraordinarily beautiful young woman. So she had the pick of the guys at Cornell. She chose

Marty Ginsburg—the first man, she said, who seemed to care that she had a brain.

Throughout her long career and 56 years of marriage, he supported her and even actively lobbied for her to get her Supreme Court nomination, and was by her side pushing for her every step of the way.

He was a very successful tax lawyer in his own right. But he saw his mission as helping his wife succeed. It's a beautiful love story, but it's also a lesson.

> **I think about how we men and women can support one another and how a partnership can really come together so it's better than the sum of its parts.**

EYE: Absolutely. I talk about her legacy, but you have created a legacy here because not only have you made an amazing film, but this is something that's going to live on for years. This is going to be for future generations and in classrooms. You've really captured a very important person in history. How do you feel about your legacy?

BETSY: I feel very lucky to have in the past decade juggled being a professor and teaching young journalists who were coming up who wanted to make documentaries and do journalistic videos, and at the same time to have done stories about groundbreaking women.

I worked on a project 10 years ago, the Makers Project, and that's how I first met Justice Ginsburg. And now to have a done a film focusing on one of the most important women of the 20th century is very rewarding,

EYE: Betsy and Julie, thank you so much. This movie is a revelation. It's educational, entertaining, and it's phenomenal. I really appreciate you joining me today.

First published in May, 2018.

Gladys Kalibbala and Jessica Yu

Award-Winning Director Jessica Yu Spotlights Heroic Journalist Gladys Kalibbala's Passion

By Patricia Caso

In *Garden of the Lost and Abandoned: An Extraordinary Story of One Ordinary Woman and the Children She Saves,* Academy Award-winning filmmaker and author Jessica Yu follows heroic Ugandan journalist Gladys Kalibbala, who uses her energy, creativity and meager resources to rescue lost and abandoned children.

Gladys' column, *Lost and Abandoned*, has drawn attention to the plight of hundreds of forsaken children. She routinely faces many difficult and dangerous situations to help them.

> "What Gladys does is hard. But the cumulative impact of her deliberate—not random—acts of kindness, and the joy she takes in them, remind us that we discover our humanity when we engage. And if we persist, things happen."
> —*Jessica Yu*

Intrigued with Gladys' life-saving deeds, I began researching more about her life and discovered Jessica Yu's own multi-faceted story. Not only was she an award-winning director in television, documentaries and films, she'd just written her first book, *Garden of the Lost and Abandoned*. And what a compelling changemaker Jessica brings to readers...

EYE: You featured Gladys Kalibbala in your film, *Misconception*, a documentary about population issues. But you had made many notable films on a variety of people before meeting Gladys—what triggered the idea to write a book about her?

JESSICA: I wanted to understand what makes her tick and to be closer to it. In making the film, we were only able to follow her for a few days. It just seemed strange to be leaving after about a week or two, so I was thinking about ways to explore this story. That's when I thought I should pursue writing a book about her.

In Uganda there are many reasons for children being lost, like illness, poverty, misfortune or simple separation from family. I was impressed by the fact that Gladys was rescuing so many children on her own. She doesn't have money, transportation or the backing of an NGO. But over the years she has taken on hundreds of these cases.

That was striking to me. At the same time, she is this cheerful, buoyant personality, who is larger than life. It's not pollyannaish. She clearly takes joy in the effort of solving these complex, intractable problems having to do with individual human beings.

EYE: I found Gladys' compassionate but steely focus fascinating. What do you hope readers will appreciate most about her?

JESSICA: I hope people come away from the book with an appreciation for what I've come to see as Gladys' optimistic pragmatism—the notion that any positive step has value. Helping individuals can be a messy, complex, no-end-in-sight proposition.

> **But Gladys shows us how quickly a person's fortune can change with even a modest intervention. I've seen her travel a whole day for a ten-minute visit, just to let a child know that she is still involved. That kind of personal contact can brighten a child's view of the world.**

What Gladys does is hard. But the cumulative impact of her deliberate—not random—acts of kindness, and the joy she takes in them remind us that we discover our humanity when we engage. And if we persist, things happen.

EYE: Many of the lost children's stories are gut-wrenching. Did you ever want to be personally involved?

JESSICA: Of course! When Gladys interviewed a young mom whose child had to drop out of school for want of a few dollars, it was not easy to be a passive observer.

> **I might provide for our travel and miscellaneous expenses related to my visits, but I could not step in and try to save the day. Gladys understood that as well. The book had to describe the reality she faces every day.**

EYE: Gladys has been described as "hard-nosed and warm-hearted." What do you see in Gladys that makes her so focused, determined and persistent?

JESSICA: Gladys took on a lot of responsibility at a young age. She was the firstborn in a family of eight children. Her father had children by more than one woman. He drank, and her parents often fought.

For several years, Gladys was sent to live with her grandparents. They were loving and generous, the kind of people who opened their house to others. If someone needed a meal, there was always room at the table.

EYE: But it got tougher than that...

JESSICA: When Gladys was 17, her grandfather died, and Gladys was left in charge of her younger siblings. She had to leave school to work, but she did not hesitate. I think those years with her grandparents gave her a grounding for the way things could be, for how we should treat each other. You could always make room at the table.

That said, she is a resourceful and creative thinker, naturally drawn to problem-solving. She finds much joy in applying her skills, experience and energy to helping others.

EYE: How do you think Gladys sees herself?

JESSICA: She has told me that this is just how she was made! She doesn't consider her altruistic bent extraordinary. To her it's just common decency.

EYE: How does Gladys support herself?

JESSICA: Alongside her work with all the cases of these kids, she realizes that she needs some way to sustain her work. She has to knock on doors, trying to scramble her way to help each one of these kids.

She doesn't have a lot of money. She doesn't always have something she can bring to the problem in a concrete way. She is, however, so creative, and so persistent that she comes up with little solutions everywhere. She took out a loan against her meager earnings at the New Vision newspaper to buy a small plot of land.

EYE: Why would Gladys want to buy a plot of land?

JESSICA: She wanted to start a farming concern, or garden, to raise money for her expanding efforts. That is why I titled the book *Garden of the Lost and Abandoned*. Gladys was trying to get this project off the ground.

> **The children are on a school break now, up to two months long, and if you don't have family to go to, it's very difficult. Some stay over at the garden and help out. They love it because it really feels like it's their place.**

EYE: So what's more rewarding for you, writing a book or directing?

JESSICA: They're different. The thing I savored in writing the book was the opportunity to follow a story without any crew, equipment or schedule. There is a different kind of focus—an intense focus—that you can achieve when you don't have worry about all those other things.

When you make a documentary, there is this goal of

being unobtrusive; you are a fly on the wall. It's an unattainable goal because you always have to worry about technical things like moving cameras around when the sun is overhead or feeding the crew.

> When you are with Gladys, by the way, you don't eat all day. It's go, go, go! With Gladys, like a lot of people in her life, I ended up trailing her in her wake and trying to absorb things as they were happening. I loved the immediacy of that and the ability to deeply watch.

EYE: I was fascinated with your unusual path to directing. You were an accomplished fencer at Yale University, competing on the U.S. team at the World Championships after college. Looking for employment with flexible hours to make extra money, you took a job on a small film.

Fast forward a few years and you are a successful director with an Oscar to boot! You are known for your wide range of subjects. You have been called "eclectic" and "humanity-driven." How would you describe yourself?

JESSICA: (laughs) I'm terrible at describing me. I always feel like that there is something external that pulls me into a certain direction. An example is meeting

Gladys. That was not something I planned or had looked forward to in pursuing a story.

> **I think some of the documentaries I worked on depict somebody who has somehow gone against the grain, created an alternate universe for themselves or discovered a different approach to their situation in order to satisfy some human need.**

I like the fact there is always some universal human impulse there. That was certainly the case with writing about Gladys in the book. There was something about her voice in my head that made me think *This makes sense. I can do this.*

EYE: What was your beginning experience like as a director?

JESSICA: When I directed my first episodic, *The West Wing*, it was through John Wells Productions. They invited me to observe and then gave me my first shot. My great motivator was fear.

There were so few women directors and there are still so few women working in that capacity. I felt like, *Oh, I'd better not blow it because then they'll never let anyone else do this.* There were a few women I met, but the numbers were so low.

In fact, on my first day to direct the episode, there was a parking space right next to the stage that said "Director" on it. I parked there. An elderly security guard came out and said, "Oh, honey, I'm sorry but that space is for the director." I said, "I know. This is weird for me, too." (laughter)

EYE: With #MeToo and the Time's Up movement, what do you think it will take to achieve the equality and respect women deserve?

JESSICA: I think this is a national conversation. Companies and people taking a stand can move this forward. Acting or not acting makes a statement. There are certainly more conversations on the sets.

> **It is important to recognize how prevalent this culture has been. Despite backlash and some resistance, the pendulum is swinging. I feel there is going to be real change. This is how change happens; it will always be a bit messy.**

EYE: On a totally different note, did you ever imagine that you would be standing on a national television stage accepting an Oscar for *Breathing Lessons: The Life and Work of Mark O'Brien* and be such a successful director?

JESSICA: No. Definitely not. Someone asked me a long time ago where I wanted to be in ten years. I said, "I basically would like to be doing what I was doing, but maybe not driving the exact same car."

> **I've been able to have projects where I feel deeply about them or I am committed to seeing them through or they are deeply satisfying. In that I feel lucky.**

EYE: Jessica, thank you so much for introducing us to Gladys. Continued success in all your meaningful pursuits, and we'll look for more of your work in theaters and television.

First published in April, 2018.

Lindsey Seavert

Reporter Lindsey Seavert Documents the Transformation of a Failing School in the Award-Winning *Love Them First*

By Patricia Caso

For a year, award-winning reporter and photojournalist Lindsey Seavert and Ben Garvin of KARE 11 in Minneapolis, Minnesota, were embedded in the challenged Lucy Laney Elementary School. They recorded the realities children of color face in that school located in the gritty, poverty-stricken area of North Minneapolis for their local station.

> "It started as a news series called *Lessons from Lucy Laney*. And it was about two stories a month. We quickly realized it's so much more than that. This should be a documentary."
>
> —*Lindsey Seavert*

Ultimately their series became the documentary *Love Them First* in which Lindsey and Ben showcased the inspirational Lucy Laney Principal Mauri Melander

Friestleben and her students tackling and determined to beat the perennial low test scores and poor academic performance, and turn the school around.

I caught up with the busy Lindsey Seavert to find out more about Mauri and what was behind the gutsy and powerful story that grew into the award-winning documentary *Love Them First*...

EYE: How did your involvement with *Love Them First* begin?

LINDSEY: I was covering the vigil for the two-year-old boy who died on the corner at Lucy Laney Elementary. Mauri, Lisa, the assistant principal, and the staff members had led every child out of the school building one by one. Each one was holding a carnation and a handwritten note for the boy who died. They formed this big, quiet, peace vigil.

> **It was largely silent, except for the voice of Mauri, who spoke to the media, "This can't be normalized in our community. And it is. And if we don't talk about it here and now and if we don't raise the alarm, no one will."**

This had followed a string of violent incidences, and the kids were scared.

EYE: What struck you about the way Mauri handled this difficult situation?

LINDSEY: She said, "A car drove by and a man pulled out a gun. Unfortunately, a bullet came out of the gun and went through little Vontaze's heart and he died." She was so sensitive but so honest.

I was struck by her honesty, and also her willingness to fight for her kids, to be this disruptor and protector in a way I hadn't seen before.

Shortly after I filed the story, I went through a difficult pregnancy and was home with my preemie for about six months. Mauri and the kids stuck in my head. I decided that when I went back to work I was going to listen to the little voice in my heart and see what story was inside that school.

EYE: How did you come to join forces with photojournalist Ben Garvin and ultimately make this film?

LINDSEY: I worked a lot with Ben Garvin, who had his own experience related to the protest in the neighborhood after the police officer-involved shooting.

He was in Lucy Laney to record a story on Thanksgiving and why kids were thankful. An announcement came over the loudspeaker that day and it was Mauri talking to the kids again in that wonderful, sensitive honesty she has about what was happening in the neighborhood and why kids were seeing helicopters and fires, and walking through scary protests on the way to school.

He had recorded that announcement because he thought, *Wow, this is amazing*. We were driving around one day on assignment and we couldn't stop talking about our own experiences in the neighborhood and in the school.

EYE: Why did you chose Mauri's voice rather than your own for the narration?

LINDSEY: I'm struck by her unflinching strength, her faith and love for her students. She also has a preacher-like quality. When she speaks, you listen and you go on a journey and are transformed. She has this quote that says, "If you're in this work, you're in it to change the world."

> **And you can see in her eyes and feel it in her heart: that is at the forefront of what she does every day. She will not stop until she changes the world for her kids.**

At the beginning of the film, there's a scene on the first day of school where the community lines up, Mauri hugs every child and they get high fives. She started that five or six years ago based on a similar event in Chicago, modeled after the Million Father March.

> **I think vulnerability is her superpower. She lets her guard down, but her strength is so apparent and inspiring.**

EYE: What were some of the challenges in making the documentary?

LINDSEY: Trust. Ben and I recognized that we were white, privileged journalists entering a high poverty, high-crime area including a "failing school." We had to be authentic.

> **We had to show diversity; we didn't want to pity or sensationalize. We listened to the community who felt strongly about showing their grittiness.**

Most schools don't let you in to see what's happening, much less a big project without an escort. But Mauri said, "You know, I would like to try this, but it's not just up to me. It's up to every single staff person in our building."

Jane Helmke, our news director, agreed because she said that as a white woman and as a news director, she had been at the station about 30 years and she felt like she had many opportunities in her lifetime to confront and combat racism in our community and she hadn't done enough. She was totally on board when we said Mauri would "tell" the story.

EYE: Were there any surprises in your filming?

LINDSEY: I think I knew this as a mother and a parent, but just how quickly the kids opened up to us, connected and how unfiltered they were. Kids are just such great truth tellers. They see right through you, right?

Mauri's announcement every day is "You are the brightest, most intelligent, definitely best-looking in all of North Minneapolis and you are worth the cost."

> **They stand straight, their heads are high, shoulders are square, chests are out. They have been told that they are worthy and they believe it.**

I surprised myself also. Some of my own stereotypes, my own expectations of what I thought an urban education was and where you can get a good high-quality education, were upended.

I think I had been somehow conditioned to believe that the school would look different, feel different, feel scarier, feel more sorrowful or sad in that lens of pity. And Lucy Laney was anything but.

EYE: It ends in a less-than-fairytale way. How did you handle that?

LINDSEY: We let the story take shape throughout the year. Test scores and attendance had been improving.

They thought they finally got off the list of failing schools. It was a big celebration. And we thought, *Well, gosh, there's our story, there's our triumphant end, hooray for education.* And so we felt really satisfied.

> **This is the perfect ending for a little school that could, and did. And then two weeks later, we got a text from the principal saying you might want to come over to the school. It was all a big mistake. And we thought, *No, no, no, no, no, no, this can't be.***

We felt so terrible for the school when a district clerical error meant they still didn't get off the list and that our documentary was ruined. Who wants to watch a story about that? We ran over to the school and people were crying. We taped a little bit.

After some time, we realized perhaps it was meant to be because we could all have a broader impact. It was the impetus for a broader conversation about standardized testing and measuring children, because everything you see inside that school is far from failing.

EYE: What do you hope audiences take away?

LINDSEY: What we've realized as we've taken *Love Them First* around the country is that it's not a North

Minneapolis story or a Minnesota story, it's an American story and an American struggle in education. How can we all work for the collective good of all of our children?

> **And I really would love people to think more deeply about standardized testing and how we measure our children. What is within our reach is our ability to make a difference for children by looking through the lens of love.**

Mauri's approach of radical love is something she's quick to say is not like touchy, lovey-love. It's love with high expectations—challenging love.

EYE: That title grabs your attention and pulls you in. Was that an automatic choice for you and Ben?

LINDSEY: We didn't know what to call this movie for a long time. I always felt very strongly that whatever we named it, there should be "love" in the title. But we had some on the team, a few documentary consultants and even Mauri, who weren't so sure about *Love Them First* as a title.

Mauri felt like people would misinterpret that. It's like, "Oh, you just love the kids and everything's going to be okay. And it's not a warm, fuzzy love. It's like the high expectations kind of love."

I like the reason I chose it, because I feel like it's actionable. Plus, those are Mauri's own words, and I felt like it was a call to the world.

EYE: You've been a reporter for 19 years. What drew you to journalism?

LINDSEY: Going back to my childhood, I've always been drawn to stories about the underdog. I was a pretty awkward child. I had crossed eyes and lots of eye surgeries and thick glasses; I was really quiet, shy and introverted. So writing was always my outlet.

Also, my parents were teachers and really encouraged a love of reading, writing and public service. I would set up a table in my living room every weekend with Jessica Savitch, one of the first women to anchor a national weekend newscast, and read stories along with her and make my dog watch me!

In college I ended up going more into print because I thought, well, television could never be for me. But, after a summer internship with CNN in Washington, D.C., that changed. I was just hooked.

> **I am a really visual thinker. I believe in the power of telling people's stories. I felt like I was doing a service. And that courses through my veins, giving me the wherewithal and the perseverance to keep going day after day.**

EYE: What kind of advice do you have for up-and-coming journalists?

LINDSEY: We need more voices in this industry, now more than ever. Follow your passions! In doing this documentary, we ran into a lot of doubt on all sides: the community, the school, the district, even within our own organization.

There was something inside me that I just knew. And I have this quiet strength about me. I wasn't going to shake my fist and raise a ruckus. But I navigated around a lot of barriers by following my own convictions.

EYE: So Mauri and the kids have had a big personal impact on you?

LINDSEY: I was attracted to Mauri's leadership and story because I, too, want to do my part to change the world. And while I can't fix the educational system or the violence in North Minneapolis, the greatest weapons I have are my words, my story and my heart.

> One girl in the film said: "You just got to hope. You can always find light in the darkest of places." Building understanding and empathy is probably one of the greatest gifts that have come out of the film.

EYE: What is next for you?

LINDSEY: I think about which stories help us understand the world we currently live in versus the world we want to live in. I'm looking for stories that create and spark empathy, stories that help people uncover their own biases and assumptions, stories that take us on a journey of the world we want to create for our children and future generations.

> I've been thinking a lot about how can I build relationships with the keepers of those stories and the people who tell them.

EYE: Thank you, Lindsey, for your time and your insights! Congratulations to you and Ben for being 2020 Alfred I. du-Pont Columbia Award winners as well. *Love Them First* is a must-see for every community! Continued success as you go forward.

First published in February, 2020.

Sarah Burns

Sarah Burns on Filmmaking, Criminal Injustice and the Central Park Five

By Stacey Gualandi

After I saw the jaw-dropping documentary *The Central Park Five*, I had to talk to the film's director, writer and producer, Sarah Burns. The film is based on Burns' book of the same name and is a riveting re-examination of the notorious 1989 assault and rape of the Central Park jogger. I wanted to learn how and why Burns decided to focus on this subject matter for her first film.

> "Ultimately, I found my way to filmmaking by finding a story I was so passionate about and thought needed to be done. I had to make this film."
> —Sarah Burns

Burns realized there was a compelling human story that needed to be told about the five teens accused, convicted and later vindicated of the crime. The film recently earned Burns a Writers Guild of America Award nomination, along with her husband David

McMahon and father Ken Burns, and has been a must-see at film festivals over the past year.

Sarah recently shared her own compelling story...

EYE: I remember this story vividly. There was so much television coverage about this being the crime of the century. You were just a young girl at the time. Do you have any recollection of this horrific case?

SARAH: I was totally unaware of this story. I was six when the crime happened, and living in rural New Hampshire. It wasn't until 2003, right after the convictions were vacated, that I learned anything about the story.

EYE: Give me the background and explain why this was such a headline-grabbing case.

SARAH: There was a group of teenagers from Harlem, Black and Latino, who went into the park the night of April 19, 1989. Some of the kids in the group harassed and assaulted joggers and cyclists in the park that night and a few were arrested as they left. A few hours later, the body of a woman was found in the park. She had been raped and beaten and was near death.

She did ultimately make a miraculous recovery, but it was a horrifying and brutal crime, and the attention immediately focused on the kids who had been in the park. The police put them under a lot of pressure and managed to get confessions, or incriminating statements, from five of the teens.

Four of those kids signed statements and went on to give videotaped statements which became the evidence used to convict them at trial, even though DNA tests came back negative and there was no other evidence to support it.

> It became this huge media story—splashed across the headlines and on national news every day. It really terrified people and seemed to be a sign of the times. New York City was falling apart.

EYE: What was going on at the time that made this crime so sensational?

SARAH: This case had a lot of elements that made it become a big story. It took place in Central Park, a place that was considered holy. There is something about crime there that particularly offends people. There also was the fact that the victim was a young white woman who worked at an investment bank—the newspapers called her the "golden girl"—and the suspects were Black and Latino teens.

You have this issue, the accusation of Black-on-White rape, which going back centuries in this country launched quite a few lynchings. And you started to hear the language of that previous time now being used to call these kids animals and beasts.

EYE: It's unreal now to think about that. But where was the evidence to support that hatred that the public felt?

SARAH: Nobody cared. It was just a good story. So they went with it and even when the evidence started coming in that contradicted their guilt, no one really cared.

EYE: Your father is well-known documentary filmmaker Ken Burns. Was this a path you thought your life would take?

SARAH: I grew up around filmmaking since it was the family business, and I certainly learned a lot from my father, but I was never sure I wanted to follow in his footsteps, career-wise. When I was in college, I thought I was going to major in film studies, but I switched to American studies, which in truth is actually the content of my dad's work.

> **Ultimately, I found my way to filmmaking by finding a story I was so passionate about and thought needed to be done. I had to make this film. For me, that was the better way to get into filmmaking.**

EYE: You were going to go to law school at one point, right?

SARAH: Yes. I first learned about the Central Park Five because I was working for a lawyer involved with the case at the time, but I never got to the point where I was sure I wanted to practice law.

EYE: So what was that "thing" that made you want to pursue this particular story?

SARAH: I was initially interested in the racism in the media coverage surrounding the 1989 crime; I wrote about it in my senior essay. I was doing an academic analysis. So a few years later, when I was thinking about writing a book, I wanted to focus on the whole story: false confessions, interrogation tactics and how does a false confession happen.

> That was the first thing I researched when I started working on the book. It's so irrational and frankly hard to understand—someone confessing to a crime they didn't commit. I needed to understand it myself so I could explain to other people how it happened.

EYE: Looking back, these five were practically railroaded!

SARAH: Absolutely. No one wanted to ask the questions because they were so sure of their guilt and didn't want to go against what they believed to be true.

EYE: You first tackled this story in your 2011 book, *The Central Park Five*. Why did you want to tell the story on film?

SARAH: The film provided us with the opportunity to tell the story in a different way than I could in the book. We could use the visuals from the time, the music from the time, but most importantly, interview the five teens to allow the audience to get to know them.

> **It gives them the chance to speak for themselves and to tell their own stories in their own words. It's something they had never been able to do before.**

I think the opportunity for them to tell their story was very appealing to them. Despite any misgivings they may have had about the media, which they are entitled to have, they liked the idea of it, but it did take some time for them to open up. I am really grateful for their generosity in sharing their stories with me.

EYE: I imagine this subject matter was intimidating, knowing how controversial it was at the time. You put yourself out there to face both positive and negative reaction. What do you think about the reaction the film has received?

SARAH: It's been a great experience, showing the film at festivals, then with the theatrical release, and then that the "Five" have been able to come to some of the screenings and engage with the audience. That has been such an amazing thing to be a part of and to witness. People see the film and they are outraged.

There have been standing ovations. I think for the "Five" it has been healing and therapeutic. They are getting the attention now.

EYE: When their convictions were vacated in 2003 after Matias Reyes came forward admitting he committed the crime, no one knew that they had been vindicated. Many have said their innocence didn't get the attention, but their guilt did.

SARAH: Yes, it was a much smaller story, and that is something we want to correct. We were trying to tell the truth about a story that not enough people know.

> **Our goal was not to get the "Five" a settlement. We did this because it's important and there are much broader lessons to be learned from it that we should all be talking about.**

EYE: What are those lessons?

SARAH: One to note is the underlying racism that allowed people to believe, without question, that these guys were guilty. You see it now in the NYPD "stop and frisk" policy that's getting a lot of attention, or with the death of Trayvon Martin. Maybe New York City has changed since 1989, but I don't think that part of the equation has changed that much.

EYE: What did you learn about yourself while making this documentary?

SARAH: It's been a wild ride and I'm not sure I've been able to process it all yet. I do like documentary filmmaking! The book was an interesting challenge, but it was a little solitary.

> **The work of making a film is a collaborative effort—in this case it was family affair—and I really enjoyed working together with my husband and my dad, the editor, the production coordinator, and the way that the film got its shape and came together.**

EYE: Do you have another project you are passionate about now, going forward?

SARAH: The three of us are working on a documentary about Jackie Robinson, not just his baseball story but his whole story and how he fits into the civil rights movement. We want to understand the arc of that movement in the twentieth century through his life.

EYE: What do you think will happen to the "Central Park Five?"

SARAH: I hope that their civil case gets resolved; it's been a long time, so it would go a long way to helping them gain closure. They are figuring out how to move forward and get their lives together and I wish them the best of luck in that.

EYE: Are you feeling empowered by helping to right an injustice?

SARAH: What's been amazing is sharing the film with audiences and the "Five," and allowing them to have this experience and the support from a large audience who wants to cheer for them and get behind them. That's what makes me feel good about this whole project.

EYE: Sarah, thank you, for shedding light on the truth about a dark moment in our history.

First published in January, 2013.

Stacey Reiss

Spaceship Earth Producer Stacey Reiss on Biosphere 2 and How Small Groups Can Make Big Change

By Stacey Gualandi

It's a pleasure to talk to my former colleague Stacey Reiss, the award-winning documentary filmmaker and producer of films like *The Eagle Huntress, The Perfection* and her new Sundance Film Festival hit *Spaceship Earth*.

It's the story of a unique ecological experiment involving eight adventurers who, in 1991, quarantined for two years inside a huge replica of the Earth's ecosystem called Biosphere 2 near Tucson, Arizona.

> It's about the power of small groups, and that they can come together to achieve great things and accomplish change.
>
> —Stacey Reiss

We have profiled Stacey many times here on *The Women's Eye*. And not only are we both former *Inside Edition* colleagues (in the early years!), we both spell our name the right way, with an E-Y. It's been a long time since we've spoken. And now all these years later, the trails she has blazed...

STACEY: We've come a long way since then. It was a good boot camp for getting started in the business. I'm currently in Park City, Utah, at my father's home. While we were here the mountain shut down, as did both L.A. and New York due to the pandemic. Rather than try to go home to New York, we decided to stay put.

EYE: You must just be heartsick when you see what's happening in New York. What is it that you say to the folks there right now?

STACEY: Well, it's really strange not being there because I got my start as a journalist there, working for many years for NBC News. I covered Hurricane Katrina, and every major news event in New York, from the blackout to 9/11.

So the idea that I'm not only not in New York, but I'm not working in news any longer is this very surreal experience. There's never been something in my lifetime on this scale. There hasn't been something like this where I haven't been in the trenches covering it.

> **In a way, it doesn't really matter where you are. We're all in this together now. It's the same experience no matter where you're located.**

EYE: Are you wishing you were covering this right now?

STACEY: Since 9/11, I've had two kids, so my perspective is very different. Right now, my perspective is making sure my children are OK and figuring out how to manage their dislocation and anxiety.

During those other events, I didn't have that same concern. So I could go put myself out there, covering something and not really think about anyone else. So it was just like a different time in my life. Now there are other people I need to be there for so that's been the challenge for me.

EYE: How is COVID-19 changing the film industry? Is this going to open the floodgates for documentaries on the pandemic?

STACEY: I don't know. I think it's very hard right now to be in production because it's not really safe to be out there filming. Most shows and production are shut down. Can you make a film about what's going on when it might not be the wisest thing to be out there on the front lines covering this?

> **From a journalist's point of view, it's really challenging. You can't go in "boots on the ground." I'm sure there'll be some exceptions. And I'm sure some projects will come out. But it remains to be seen what will actually come out of this.**

EYE: So it's been a real challenge?

STACEY: I don't know any of my colleagues who have not been hit by this in some way. I went to Sundance with *Spaceship Earth,* and we were really lucky to premiere it there.

The film was purchased by Neon as a theatrical distributor. They recently won three Academy Awards for *Parasite*.

If you asked me who I wanted to buy the movie going into Sundance, it would have been Neon! Every other film festival, for the most part, that I was invited to after that, was postponed or canceled. The whole film festival landscape has really changed.

EYE: The last time we interviewed you, you had said as a producer, I'm quoting you, *you need to be nimble, a good problem solver and open to change.*

STACEY: I always have five balls in the air. I'm trying to not let any of them fall, but I'm also realistic that there are projects that will be at different stages. Some will happen. Some won't.

I just got involved in starting to do some scripted work. I produced my first narrative film last year—*The Perfection* on Netflix—and I have been working on a new project. And I've also optioned a book with another director for another scripted project.

I have a number of other projects that are in pre-production in the early stages. We're getting treatments and sizzle reels together, all the things we can. The moment that someone says, "Great. Go!" we'll be ready.

EYE: You do such an amazing job with the different types of stories and people you find. Documentaries are now becoming almost our best friend. How are those now becoming even more essential in this climate?

STACEY: I think right now people are consuming content in a way they never have before. I'm very caught up on documentary viewing and I've sent out lists of a lot great documentaries to watch with your kids, by yourself or with your partner. I'm happy people are watching so many documentaries.

EYE: Speaking of lists, *Spaceship Earth* has already been put on a list of one of the best documentaries of 2020 so far. Congratulations! Are you surprised?

STACEY: I'm always happy when I make a list. I love a good list. That was really exciting! When we got into Sundance documentary competition, we were overjoyed with that news. I'm not surprised in that it's a story that I think people kind of remember.

If you google "Biosphere 2," which actually still exists in Arizona, you find out it's this enormous glass terrarium, which is an incredible structure.

> It's very sci-fi looking. There's never been a film about it before. So a lot of people were very excited to understand it.

EYE: Why do you think it is so timely right now?

STACEY: This story is about eight people who live inside a closed system for two years. So if we feel all cooped up with cabin fever after two or three weeks, think about them being there for two years, doing work to study the environment and what it would be like in a closed system or for life on another planet. It could not be more relevant right now.

When you're in something, it's very hard to see it in a rearview mirror. I do not think I would ever ask for us to experience what we're going through right now, but it felt like our planet needed a reset.

> These people who were in Biosphere 2 were onto this idea of climate change very early. They could see this 25 years ago. They were studying it. And now we can't ignore it.

EYE: What was your goal in making this film pre-COVID?

STACEY: It was so people would see this and see the work these people did. Hopefully people would change their behavior, change their actions.

We could learn a lot from this work that was done then and in many cases forgotten. One of the most beautiful parts about Sundance is we brought some of the people who were involved in that experiment.

EYE: Did you really feel a sense that you were a part of the Biosphere yourself? Did you get a sense of what it must have been like?

STACEY: Every film you make is about a team of people who came together and pulled something off. No matter how many times you make a film, it presents new challenges, new personalities.

That's one of the greatest things about making films; it's like everyday problem solving. *OK, this happened.*

What am I going to do about it? You have to figure it out.

I like to tease Matt Wolfe, the director, that for two years we went into our own Biosphere and luckily we came out and we're still friends. We're actually collaborating and brainstorming other projects. I guess it was very much its own Biosphere.

EYE: It wasn't a perfect experiment. When you put a bunch of humans together in a space like that, things are going to go wrong. It's human nature. What is it that you think people should take away from this film?

STACEY: It all started with a small team; they were innovators and disruptors. I hope younger people will realize that even though they're just one person or in a small group of people, that big things can happen out of that.

> **I think that we need those fresh perspectives and innovators to give us some new ideas about how to face the challenges that are ahead of us.**

EYE: We hope we all can learn something from what we are going through with COVID-19. I imagine there are going to be things that will emerge out of this situation that will change our future. Is that how you look at what we're going through right now?

STACEY: It's really hard to say because it's so early into it. But there have been silver linings for me, like spending more time with my family. I travel a lot doing the work that I do.

> **I think it's making all of us appreciate the things we miss right now, the things we can't do right now that we take for granted like our health, our communities, the elderly population and planet.**

I hope there's that shift in perspective and people can look at it as a reset and that when we all get to go back outside, we'll go back with different intentions and a different appreciation of the things we really miss.

EYE: What would you like to work on after this COVID-19 world?

STACEY: There are three things I normally think about when I'm deciding about projects:

1) I think about the team of people that I want to work with and be in constant communication with.

2) In terms of subject matter, it's about a project I want to think about all the time,

so I can only take it on if I'm OK with it taking over my dreams, taking over my Sunday afternoon thoughts. I really want to be engaged with it. I want to feel like I'm really connected to the material.

3) I love to travel to places I've never been before. I know when the director of the *Eagle Huntress* contacted me, I said, "Wow, Mongolia! I'm going to shoot in Mongolia!" As soon as someone says it's OK to travel again, I will be the first person to book my flight to wherever.

So I have hope for the doctors who are working on a vaccine. That's what I mean by a small group of people coming together, now hopefully from all different countries around the world, to try to solve this together.

EYE: Thank you for your small group work efforts over the years, Stacey, because your body of work is amazing. I can't wait to see what's in the future for you.

First published in April, 2020.

Part II
Photographers: Filming Their Subjects

"The camera is an instrument that teaches people to see without a camera."

—*Dorothea Lange*, Documentary Photographer and Photojournalist

Heidi Levine

Combat Photojournalist Heidi Levine on Covering Deadly War Zones

By Pamela Burke

I stumbled upon a fascinating article about female conflict photographers in *American Photo* recently, and couldn't take my eyes off a powerful photo of Syrian women crossing the border into Jordan shot by Heidi Levine.

It became a TWE Photo of the Week, and the beginning of a journey to find Heidi and interview her for the website. Her photos from some of the world's most volatile war zones are unforgettable slices of life, the images so real that you think you are there.

> "My only explanation of why I do this would be to say I can best describe this drive as a sort of 'calling.' It really makes me who I am."
>
> —*Heidi Levine*

Heidi surfaced in Israel, residing in a building where Jews and Arabs live together. It was important for her to live in this mixed neighborhood, she says, because it exposes her children to people from two very different backgrounds living side by side in peace.

There were many questions to ask this mother of three who is one of a special breed of female photographers covering areas of conflict in many parts of the world...

EYE: You have been called one of today's top female conflict photographers. You've taken photographs of dangerous riots and documented some of the world's most explosive war zones. What drives you to put yourself in these kinds of situations?

HEIDI: I have always been interested in helping people. When I was a kid, I volunteered and worked with children who had cognitive disabilities, as a Candy Striper in a hospital at the age of 14, with the elderly in their homes and in a nursing home and worked on a suicide hotline.

I was also obsessed with learning about underprivileged neighborhoods in the Boston and New York area. My father would take me along on a business trip to New York City and point me in the direction of a museum, but I would sneak off to Harlem.

I was obsessed with studying sociology and psychology and really thought at the time I would become a sociologist or psychologist. I also dreamed of becoming a doctor.

EYE: Do you think taking photographs became an extension of this desire to help people, but in a different way?

HEIDI: In many ways all these experiences have been incorporated in the way I have tried to use the power of photography as my best tool to help others and make a difference. It would be difficult to understand the force that drives me into the epicenter of a conflict zone even when my own editors are advising me not to go.

> **I can honestly say, there have been moments when I wished I were stopped because, yes, it is scary and dangerous.**

EYE: What made you decide you would make photojournalism your career? And how did you get involved in the conflict arena?

HEIDI: Both my parents are very creative people. They were young when I was born, just barely 20 years old themselves, and very hard-working. My father was passionate about photography and for a period of time was working as a manager in a camera store.

He bought me my first camera and we would spend time together walking around Boston taking photographs. I took a photography class in high school, but

I was a bit of a rebel and was not as interested in taking pictures of still life as I was of taking pictures of people. The *Boston Globe* and their incredible display of images from around the world heavily influenced me.

EYE: When did you begin to develop your talent and expertise as a photographer?

HEIDI: At the University of Massachusetts in Amherst I worked as a photographer for the school newspaper, the *Daily Collegian*, and took my first journalism classes with Dr. Frank Faulkner.

> He was one of those great teachers in my life who really made a difference. He was also a working journalist and a Vietnam vet who had worked as a journalist during the war.

He told me that of all the students at that time, I really reminded him most of himself. When I went to Israel the first time during a summer break just to be on a kibbutz for six weeks and travel, I called the Associated Press in Israel from the contact I got from the *Boston Globe* picture editor.

After an interview that resulted in a job offer, I called my professor from a phone booth and asked his advice. He told me to grab the opportunity and that I would learn much more by actually working than by learning in class. It was that one phone call and his advice that set me on this path.

EYE: You seem to have been a risk-taker from a young age.

HEIDI: I also have a funny connection to the *Boston Globe*. I had my first front page of the *Globe* as a small kid, but not as a photographer. My parents took me to a dog show in Boston and I climbed into one of the dog cages.

A *Globe* photographer captured the moment, and it was published on the first page. I guess I have been blessed to both be the subject on a front page and have my photographs published. Maybe it shows that from a very young age, it was in my blood to take risks.

I really got a great training at the AP. I got to do everything. I worked in the lab, edited and captioned pictures of others as well as my own and dealt with their subscribers. At the time I thought I would stay in the region for a year or two, not half of my life. The Israeli-Palestinian conflict was my first encounter with covering conflict, and remains my most intimate.

EYE: Did you have any particular mentors along the way, or photographers you admired who inspired you to pursue this career?

HEIDI: Many photographers along the way influenced me. I have always admired Robert Capa, Henri Cartier-Bresson, Eugene Smith, Dorothea Lange, Margaret Bourke-White, Don McCullin, Nick Ut, Sebastião Salgado, James Nachtway and others.

I was surrounded by outstanding peers from the start, such as Ron Haviv, Chris Morris, Les Stone, Alfred Yaghobzadeh, Alexandra Avakian, Alexandra Boulat, Ami Vitali, and Jerome Delay—and was married to a photographer who covered conflict himself.

My boss at AP, Max Nash, was an amazing teacher who would tell me his own stories every day about covering Vietnam and working with Eddie Adams. I actually cooked him dinner when he came here. I was really blessed to meet and become friends with photographers and journalists from all over the world who are both experienced and new in the profession.

> **Everyone is tied together by this same drive inside of him or her, to try to expose what is happening and ideally try to make a difference.**

EYE: "Conflict" photojournalism is not a profession that has historically been populated by women. Was it a struggle for you to be taken seriously in the beginning?

HEIDI: Yes, it was difficult. At the start I had to fight for it because I was also very young at the time, not just because I was a woman. When I wanted to go to Lebanon to cover the refugee crisis following the Lebanon-Israel war, I was very young.

My boss did not want me to be exposed to danger because I had not yet become a mother. Later, once I was a mother, many felt it was irresponsible to place myself in danger because I was a mother.

I had to fight my way in and then fight my way to be accepted into a profession that was, and still is to some degree, very much a boys' club. In Libya, one Italian journalist I know shouted at me, "Hey, what are you doing here, you have children!" but he did not shout at any of the males. For the most part, the men I work with truly respect what I do.

EYE: Has being female worked to your advantage in some shooting situations? Does it give you better entrée when you are dealing with women and children who are sometimes in precarious positions?

HEIDI: Yes, it has given me more of an advantage for the intimate way I try to work than a disadvantage, especially when covering cultures that have strict modesty rules such as in the Middle East and beyond. I am accepted into the bedroom of a woman in mourning more easily because I am a woman.

I try my best to bond with the people I am documenting, and being a woman and even explaining that I am also a mother, often helps people trust me.

Sometimes, I am a bit of a novelty for people to meet in a war zone, so they try to protect me and offer me a place to stay. Regardless of how bad the situation is, even if their home has been bombed to the ground, they offer me something to drink.

EYE: How close will you get to the action? In some of your photos, particularly those from Libya, it looks like you are positioned very near explosions, fire and gunfire.

HEIDI: Looking back on that day, I was lucky to be unharmed; it was too close. One truckload of ammunition caught on fire, causing a large explosion, and others were flying aimlessly in all directions. At one point, I heard the whistling of a shell and could feel its incredible heat heading towards me.

I ran, not looking back, running with the memories of every burn victim I had ever seen in my entire life, just hoping not to become the next burn victim.

On other occasions we would just hit the ground. In the desert, you have no protection, yet it is safer because a heavily populated area under bombardment turns into deadly shrapnel. On my second trip to Libya, I covered Tripoli. We followed a group of rebels who were fighting the last forces still trying to resist defeat; we went right into a building.

I was with other photographers and we were capturing images of the rebels firing in a stairwell just behind them when one of the rebels was shot dead by a sniper right in front of us. The loud crackling of gunfire brought greater confusion. I was lucky, we were all lucky, not to have been hit ourselves by the sniper.

EYE: We are all lucky to see your great work. Thanks so much for sharing your photographs and your sometimes-terrifying experiences, Heidi. Good luck to you in every challenge you face in the field.

First published in June, 2013.

Photo student and Karen Shell

Photographer Karen Shell on Keeping Kids in Focus with a Camera Lens

By Catherine Anaya

Karen Shell is the founder and the executive director of Kids in Focus in Phoenix, Arizona, an innovative nonprofit she created in 2012. Once she emerged from an abusive and challenging homelife as a child, Karen found the need to reach out and empower others.

> "When you go through extreme challenges and traumas, there's no way it won't change you. But you get to choose how; I term it 'bitter or better.' I wanted to make my life better. And I didn't really know how I was going to do it."
>
> —*Karen Shell*

And better she made it! After years of working with at-risk youth, this professional photographer created Kids in Focus, showing young people how to use a camera and how photography could make a difference in their lives. Her mentor-based programs inspire them and lead to life-changing improvements in behavior, attitude and self-confidence.

I wanted to find out more about Karen's unique program and how she got her own inspiration...

EYE: I want to start by talking about your relationship with at-risk youth. It started back in the early '90s. What was it that personally drove you and your heart back in the early '90s to make volunteering and mentoring these kids such a priority in your life?

KAREN: I don't think I really knew what was driving me, but I was very clearly driven in my early '20s; something was pushing me to give back. I very actively sought out ways to do that. I look back on it now and I realize I just wanted to be happy.

> **I came to discover that giving back was very healing for me, and it kept my priorities in balance. It's very easy to get wrapped up in your own little bubble, and when you're in that bubble, all your little problems are so magnified.**

But when you give back, it's this amazingly effective way to get yourself out of that bubble and put all your problems back into perspective. So it was doing that for me all those years.

EYE: I should mention that you are a commercial photographer by trade. You went the extra mile in your volunteer efforts creating projects for at-risk children.

You coordinated Picture Day for 20 years, where you provided free school portraits for up to 1,000 homeless kids each year. What kind of shift do you see when you become closer to these kids in that kind of way?

KAREN: That particular project was really effective. It's basically giving them dignity. And when I introduced bringing stylists in as well as the photographers, it really became evident to me how much dignity it was giving those kids.

> **But really, all the work I've been doing over the years just comes down to connection, giving these kids an opportunity to connect with an adult in a healthy way and build trust. That is what so many of those kids lack.**

EYE: Let's talk about Kids in Focus, because trust and that mentorship are really the foundation of what you do. You've said you feel that your whole life has been about preparing you to create Kids in Focus back in 2012. What was that first project about? What kind of impact did it make not just on them, but on you personally?

KAREN: The kids who experienced the first Kids in Focus projects were ones I had already been mentoring for five years. So I knew them very well, but was not mentoring them in any kind of photographic way. I was just hanging out in class with them, helping set up reading programs, helping the teacher.

The kids were at so many different reading levels. I was providing Christmas for them, whatever I could do just to be there and spend time with them. So this project, which became Kids in Focus, was just another one of my many ideas. I'm an idea creator.

I really had no idea what was going to come from it. I thought I'd get some photographers I know and we'd teach the kids some photography and we'd put on an exhibit of their work—that would probably boost their confidence.

So when I finished that project, I could not believe my eyes because these kids whom I knew well were drastically different. They were more connected; they were more competent, just life-changing transformations.

EYE: So did that come from the photography itself? Or did it come from the mentorship or a combination of the above?

KAREN: It's the combination with the camera, which is a really safe way for these kids to reconnect. When kids go through trauma, they disconnect from what's happening, from the people around them, from the environments and ultimately from themselves.

> The camera for some reason is incredibly safe. Without the camera, they will not look around. And some of them literally resist it. They don't want to connect with that...that painful world out there. They would rather stay in here. The camera gives them a safety net.

All the mentors are trained photographers. So we pair them with a mentor who is trained to see and to notice. And then we build that trust in those relationships and we take them on field trips all over the Valley.

That gives them an opportunity to experience less stressful environments and lets them practice the authentic, playful versions of themselves. And then on top of that, we celebrate every project in a culmination where the kids can show their work, whether it's at a giant public exhibit opening or it's just for the for the school or their local community. It gives them an immense sense of pride.

EYE: How surprised were you to see that kind of result? Were you expecting to see that kind of shift?

KAREN: I was absolutely not expecting it. It was really kind of by accident. But when I finished that first project, I thought, *This is it. I finally have found the way to really make a difference in these kids' lives.* That's when I focused all my energies into this one program, and it has been growing ever since.

EYE: I want to talk about the kids in particular when they come to you. What kinds of challenges are they facing and what age group do you interact with?

KAREN: We start with kids at ten and we are working with kids who are now technically into adulthood at eighteen and nineteen. We also have grad programs that keep the kids involved.

> **These kids have experienced homelessness, neglect, abuse, poverty, serious illness— all sorts of major traumas.**

EYE: Where do you find these kids?

KAREN: We reach them through partner organizations. They provide a place to meet with the kids, and in most cases, transportation for the field trips. Our current partners are Boys and Girls Clubs where kids are living in very low-income areas, also Children First Leadership Academy, where 100% of the student population is living at or below the poverty line and the majority are homeless, also various foster care organizations, Phoenix Children's Hospital. I can go on and on.

EYE: Do these kids need to first demonstrate their desire to be a part of these programs or do you just accept anyone and hope they get the results you want them to get?

KAREN: I'm so glad you asked that question, because a really important part of this project for me is teaching kids as many life lessons as possible as long as I've got their attention. An important part of that is teaching them accountability and responsibility.

So these kids apply to get into the program with an application that they fill out. They also have to sign a contract that they will respect themselves and others and that they will keep their grades up. And many other things.

> **Just the thought of them not being in the program is enough to change these kids' behavior. I've never had to kick a child out.**

EYE: We've talked about the transformation we see with these kids. What kind of transformation has it made for you?

KAREN: You know I didn't even realize the power photography had in my own life. And now seeing these kids respond so well helps me realize what it was doing for me all those years. There's a powerful value in learning to see outside of oneself.

> **Little did I know all those years that's what it was doing for me. This program gives me an immense purpose. My entire journey has been grooming me to do this, but it has not been without a lot of sacrifice.**

It's been difficult at every level financially. In every aspect of my life, I've made a lot of sacrifices and sometimes I think I must be crazy. But then I see the results in these kids and I see their lives change long-term.

And I say to myself, *How could I not do this?* I've just got to keep the faith that it's all going to work out...I'm not going to end up on the streets. And that the sacrifices are all worth it.

EYE: Speaking of faith, it's been eight years since that first project. And I personally feel like Kids in Focus is on the brink of an explosion. So where would you like to see Kids in Focus go from where it is now?

KAREN: I feel the same thing. I want to reach more kids because I absolutely believe in the life-changing value of this program. I would like to go statewide and then regional and national—so we're working on doing it, even to have international components where we pair the kids with kids in another country.

We get mentors over there to work with those kids and then the kids can share their lives and introduce some global understanding and tolerance into the program. I have lots of ideas.

EYE: You're an idea factory. You are located in Phoenix, Arizona. And when you say you want to go statewide and then beyond, that would be initially across Arizona. You say you need photographers. Are you looking for a specific kind of photographer, or is it just anyone who's willing to give their time?

KAREN: Anyone who's willing to give their time. What we're teaching these kids is basic photography—shutter speed, aperture, nothing technical whatsoever. We're simply teaching these kids to see things in a new way.

> **Anyone who can be thrown into an environment and come up with something creative is more than qualified. It's really more about their ability to connect with kids.**

EYE: What a beautiful thing you are doing with these kids and for the community. I just so applaud you and thank you very much for talking with me.

First published in October, 2019.

Mimo Khair

Global Photographer Mimo Khair Captures the Common Thread of Humanity

By Patricia Caso

Mimo Khair's global photography struck me as stunning, emotional and captivating—whether it is still life, on the streets, with children or adults. I happened upon her unforgettable pictures while scrolling through news sites on the internet.

> "I love people, and photographing them is for me a way of bringing us all closer together…I strive to create art that can 'do something.'"
>
> —*Mimo Khair*

Wanting to know more about this talented Lebanese-American photographer, wife and mother who now resides in Shanghai, China, I tracked down Mimo through email.

I found an inspirational artist who is always looking to capture the connection in our humanity, hoping the viewer is moved by it as well…

EYE: I read that you grew up during the Civil War years in a small village in North Lebanon. Did that experience play into what you look for in your street photography and documentary photos?

MIMO: I think we are a culmination of our life experiences from the moment of birth or even conception. The first twelve years of life are, as we all know, very formative, and my early years still echo strongly in everything I do.

Growing up during the civil war created resilience in me as well as a renewed value for life and all that is good in it. I am caught by moments of human emotion, beauty, strength, sadness, humanity and love.

EYE: What were you planning to do with your life before you went to New York City?

MIMO: In Lebanon, girls were mostly expected to study, conform to rules of a conservative society and take their back seat in a male-dominant world. As soon as I reached adulthood in Lebanon I felt a very strong urge to break free from a binding situation and to be able to express myself without the hammer of judgment.

> Having an American mother, I was lucky to have the option of moving to New York. I moved against all odds and threw myself into a new, strange and fantastic world at age 20.

EYE: What made you pick up a camera in 1995? And, what was your first photo?

MIMO: I came upon an old Pentax camera during a trip to New Zealand. It felt like destiny and I knew I would be doing a lot with that beautiful piece of machinery. My first photo was of Karekare's black sand beach in New Zealand.

I went back there last year and photographed my 10-year-old daughter, Lea, on the very same beach.

EYE: What captured your imagination when you started taking pictures?

MIMO: My first serious photography trip was in Egypt. It is safe to say that everything there captivated me, from the pyramids and sphinx of Giza to the magnificent temples and tombs, the beautiful Nile, the people, the light, the desert—all of it really.

EYE: How do you choose your subjects and do they always cooperate?

MIMO: When I am in the street, I allow myself to react to the environment. I mostly do not preplan my shots, but wait for situations to present themselves to me. It is a very organic process, and the subjects appear as the minutes unfold.

I find that a smile goes a very long way, as well as warmth and a genuine interest in other peoples' lives.

When you do this for a long time, you become more and more sensitive to people and able to sense who will be receptive to being photographed. I love people, and photographing them is for me a way of bringing us all closer together.

EYE: Why has street photography become such a passion for you?

MIMO: The subject, light, emotion, communication, composition, movement, and rhythm are some of the factors that can combine to create a wonderful image. It is different each time, and this is what makes street photography such an amazing style to explore.

EYE: Your captions are terrific. Is writing equally important to you?

MIMO: Yes. I believe that words complement the image and can impart another level to the image that is personal to the photographer. I put it out without any expectation of it to be accepted as part of the image, but it makes me happy to combine the two forms of art.

EYE: You conduct workshops. Do you have advice for aspiring photographers?

MIMO: Teaching photography on a regular basis keeps me motivated to continue learning myself. And I love to see others getting inspired to break barriers in their photographic journey.

The best advice I can give is to do more and more of what you love. I tasked myself with a 365 project where I took photos and posted the best one from each day with a small writing on my blog.

> **I did that for two years and it was very instrumental in my discipline as a photographer. I always advise people to try a discipline like that to get more hours of experience built into their journey.**

EYE: Can cell phones be good for taking better-than-ordinary pictures? Is there any way to take a good "selfie"?

MIMO: I believe any camera is a good camera if you love what you are doing. The mobile phone camera ensures that you always can practice your art no matter where you are.

Some of the images out there are stunning and very inspiring. I do enjoy creating "selfies" in the way of image diary entries, especially reflection shots that can combine the reflection with the environment to make a mosaic of impressions.

EYE: Do you think a photograph can make more of an impact than a video or the written or spoken word?

MIMO: A photograph can make an impact very differently. I would not say more. I believe that a photograph can act as an anchor point from which our imagination can propel us into uncharted territories of the mind.

A video is more of an usher that takes you on its predetermined journey. Similarly, words hold your hand and take you along. There is more mystery for me in an image. Like a painting or other visual arts, it allows for a lot more mind exploration and dreaming.

EYE: What or who inspires you?

MIMO: I believe that inspiration comes from all forms of art and not just photography. Sometimes when I am reading a book I find myself taking a note to create a specific photograph. Cinematic lighting is most inspiring and I find myself watching it repeatedly to learn about light.

I am always looking at the works of old and modern masters to try and see what they saw.

Art is for me an entity that moves between us all in all that we do, and the more we see, the better we understand it.

EYE: In traveling to some remote and dangerous places, did you ever feel like you were in danger? How do you prepare for those assignments?

MIMO: The most dangerous place I traveled to was the Democratic Republic of Congo to interview child soldiers and street children. I had to be in an armored car while in the streets and I was not free to walk the streets on foot as I am used to.

It did feel threatening at times, but I was completely immersed in the chase of my story and images. That excitement certainly overshadowed any sense of danger. The trip to Congo was hugely assisted by the United Nations and I could not have done it in any other way.

I mostly prepare in advance for a journey of this kind, but on some occasions, as I did with the refugee camps in Lebanon, I just walked in unassisted and on an impulse.

EYE: With your travels far and wide and now that you are living in Shanghai, what have you learned?

MIMO: I think moving around the planet and meeting more and more people, observing different cultures and customs has helped me see the human race in a different light.

> **We clothe our conflicts with causes of religion, race, country and political agendas, but in the end, people are people.**

No matter where I have been, there is a common thread of humanity that is so bright, no amount of darkness can put it out.

EYE: What common traits among people have you found?

MIMO: Simple humanity. Kindness is the same everywhere you go; love between a parent and child has many faces, but it is the same at its core.

When I capture a look in the eyes, a smile or an intense emotion, location becomes a secondary consideration.

EYE: What has been the biggest change in the world you've seen since you began your career?

MIMO: The most striking change for me is how small the world has become and how much more connected or disconnected we can all be inside of it.

I think that art in general and photography in particular have become widely accessible and, when used correctly, can be powerful tools for making the world a better place.

EYE: Do you have a mission with your photography?

MIMO: I strive to create art that can "do something." I believe that we humans are meant to give expression to the essences of art in everything that we do and that we love doing.

EYE: Do you have a favorite story about any one of your pictures? Which was your most difficult picture to get so far?

MIMO: One of my favorite stories has to do with a Polaroid photograph I took of an old lady from the Yi minority in Yunnan. I photographed her and gave her the image, but she kept returning it to me with a nod and a smile.

After several attempts and a translation, I found out that she had no idea that the photo was hers. She actually had no idea or interest in knowing what she looked like. I found that stunning to realize in this day and age of compulsive selfies.

I can't think of images that were difficult, but perhaps images of sadness or misery. I always tend to back away from and opt not to display the misfortune of others for the sake of my art unless I can manage to show the positive side of humanity that is hidden in the image.

EYE: Are your husband and young daughter your ultimate critics?

MIMO: During the time that I did my 365 project, my husband was extremely instrumental in choosing my photo of the day.

He was almost always spot-on. My daughter is a very straightforward and honest critic. If she does not like it, I am sure to know it.

EYE: What are your current and future photo projects?

MIMO: I am researching the ethnic minorities of China currently, and I plan to take several more trips to complete my project.

> **I dream of taking long photographic journeys into uncharted territories, having the luxury of spending months rather than weeks, creating beautiful books that combine writing and imagery woven together to tell a tale.**

EYE: Have you taken your best picture yet?

MIMO: No. I will keep searching for it till the end.

EYE: Your photographs stir emotions in hopeful, thoughtful, and beautiful ways! Much success to you and thanks for sharing your time, thoughts and pictures.

First published in October, 2014.

Part III
Journalists: Reporting on Their Worlds

"Journalism at its best and most effective is education."

—*Martha Gellhorn*, War Correspondent and Journalist

Carlotta Gall

Pulitzer Prize-Winning War Journalist Carlotta Gall on Getting the Story Right

By *Patricia Caso*

For twenty years British journalist Carlotta Gall covered the volatile conflicts in Chechnya, Kosovo, Serbia and other war-torn countries. She spent the last dozen years reporting from Afghanistan and Pakistan, winning a Pulitzer Prize for her work at the *New York Times* in 2009.

> "All reporting should be about the humanity. I did learn early on that wars are all about the people. They are not about the generals ordering in the tanks. They are about what the tanks crushed in their way as they went forward."
>
> —*Carlotta Gall*

Carlotta takes on a controversial subject in her latest book, *The Wrong Enemy: America in Afghanistan 2001-2014*, where she questions whether Afghanistan should have been the target for war.

I was fascinated and excited to speak with Carlotta about her dedication toward her profession. She has a passion for getting the story right from the front lines while facing tremendous danger...

EYE: The *New York Times* called your book a "searing expose of Pakistan's involvement in the Afghan War." You wrote that "Pakistan, not Afghanistan, has been the true enemy." How did you come to that conclusion?

CARLOTTA: When other reporters went off to Iraq, I stayed in Afghanistan. In 2002-2005, I traveled freely and spoke to so many people that it became clear to me that Pakistan had not stopped in its support for the Taliban.

By 2006, I remember becoming very alarmed at the scale of their venture. It was suddenly incredibly dangerous for all of us and for the NATO troops coming in.

> It looked like half the country, the south, would be back in the hands of the Taliban. That's when I realized that Pakistan's aim was far grander than I had originally thought.

EYE: You say you were aware that bin Laden was a threat before 9/11. You write that "according to one inside source, the Pakistani Intelligence (ISI) actually ran a special desk assigned to handle the al Qaeda leader." What led you to those discoveries?

CARLOTTA: I knew bin Laden was in Afghanistan and doing great damage there well before the September 2001 attacks. I was reporting from the Balkans for the *New York Times* on 9/11. When I saw the plane go into the second tower I said, "That's bin Laden."

I actually knew enough at the time of what was going on. I knew he was trouble. I'd been in Chechnya where the same group of Arabs had been coming in and causing radicalism and trouble. So I was better versed than many journalists.

> **I knew the connection with Pakistan, but knowing that bin Laden was the mastermind mainly resulted from reporting from the ground for so long.**

And, that kind of reporting made the difference in connecting the dots to uncovering Pakistan's aid to bin Laden.

EYE: What do you want readers to take away from *The Wrong Enemy*?

CARLOTTA: I really wanted to tell the whole tale of the Afghan War so that people who come later, especially younger people who might not have been alive during 9/11 or during the war, can understand from start to finish what happened. I feel I offer something important, which was witnessing everything—being there.

Also, I want readers to understand more about President Hamid Karzai, who I think is now getting a very hard time. Of course he is not perfect. What leader is flawless? I felt I needed to give the Afghans a voice.

EYE: What is the hardest reality for the Afghan people now?

CARLOTTA: It's been a long hard slog for everyone concerned in the intervention there. But, when the troops leave, the aid will be cut, the embassies will diminish their staffs and the financial assistance to Afghanistan's budget diminishes. It is such an incredibly poor country, which cannot support itself.

> **If all that declines, they will be prey to both Pakistan and Iran, their neighbors who are very predatory. The whole effort of these last 12 years will be lost, and that shouldn't happen.**

There have been advances for women, education and even the inspiration for a better life. They worked hard for it because they believed they could achieve it.

They are halfway there. So it worries me that the West could easily just turn away again. I believe that would be catastrophic.

EYE: You are certainly no stranger to war reporting. You posted reports and wrote books on the Chechnya war in the late 1990s. How well prepared were you for the type of personal physical violence you've encountered on assignment? You've been betrayed, harassed, assaulted, and even punched!

CARLOTTA: When Pakistani intelligence agents broke into my room in Pakistan, and the guy punched me wanting my handbag, I kind of resisted, which you are not supposed to do. He slammed his fist into my face.

I absolutely didn't see it coming. I went down straightaway, right down on the coffee cups and everything. I was not prepared. It was not one of my better moments. So I'm not well-prepared. I've never taken a self-defense course.

When it comes to actual war reporting, most of us get hardship courses where you get all the basics on how to look after yourself in a war zone. When I took the course, I'd already been covering Chechnya for several years.

So much of it you learn as you go along, and it's common sense. You also pick up great advice from more seasoned journalists whom you meet along the way.

EYE: What went through your mind when you heard about journalist Kathy Gannon's wounding, and photographer Anja Niedringhaus' death in Afghanistan?

CARLOTTA: It was heartbreaking. Those were two people who really knew what to do and how to handle themselves in a war. It could have been me. Any one of us could have been going to an outlying province to witness the elections and expose any problems or difficulties. I said, "Oh, my God, how could it have happened to them?"

> **When you are out there, you drop all competition; you look out for each other and work together. It was dreadful news to get. Thank goodness Kathy is on the mend. But it's a great loss to lose Anja, who was so talented and so hardworking.**

EYE: Where do you get your nerves of steel?

CARLOTTA: I'm quite a calm person, which has a lot to do with low blood pressure and just being pretty slow in the morning. It's actually the profession of following the story, getting your teeth into it and wanting to find out what happened that keeps you going. You're so busy with all that.

One of my greatest concerns is for the safety of the people who work with me like local reporters, translators, drivers, fixers, etc. They remain after you fly out. So you are often thinking about how to protect them, how to avoid giving away sources, etc. It's all involved in the reporting.

EYE: How did you decide on a career as a war correspondent?

CARLOTTA: I didn't. It just happened. I was increasingly drawn to current affairs and politics. When I did join my first newspaper, the *Moscow Times*, I was fascinated when the war started in Chechnya and I asked to go.

It was really when I got there and found I could manage on the ground and get the story filed, which was incredibly difficult in Russia in those days. You had to run around looking for a telephone exchange and dictate on the line. When I found I could do it, they kept sending me.

> **In the end I felt that if people are dying or governments are prepared to kill their own citizens to achieve aims, that is one of the most wrong things in the world. I had to write about it, expose that and show what was happening.**

EYE: How would a young person start in a war reporting career?

CARLOTTA: Go to a foreign country, preferably one where you speak the language so you don't have problems with translation. Work for a local newspaper. I went to work for the *Moscow Times* speaking Russian. Everything was opening up from the Soviet Union in the Yeltsin years. We were all young graduates who spoke Russian, so we worked with Russian journalists as well.

We were all running around all over the place, just getting these amazing stories. Since it was a national newspaper, you are straightaway writing about Yeltsin going to war in Chechnya on the front page. That was incredibly exciting, as well as a baptism by fire.

With Twitter, online websites and blogs, today's youth have even more possibilities. I think in the end the tenets of good journalism are the same. Get the story and get it right.

EYE: What is the best advice you received?

CARLOTTA: I usually keep this secret. But, because of what happened to Kathy and Anja, it is fresh in my mind. A Chechnyan commander who got it from his grandfather, who escaped Stalin's purges, once told me: "Never tell anyone where you are going or where you've come from."

It was really advice to escape kidnapping of foreigners, but also to evade enemies in war. So far I've survived and use it today.

EYE: What have you learned about yourself as a war reporter?

CARLOTTA: People say war correspondents are old hacks and are very cynical. I found you get more vulnerable to your feelings as you go along. Each case of human suffering you see just reminds you of the other ones. It can build up until it's almost overwhelming.

EYE: How do you deal with that?

CARLOTTA: You have to take a break, stop that type of reporting, turn to something else, go on holiday or do some editing instead of war reporting. You have to pace yourself. Or read.

I always keep one of Martha Gellhorn's books close at hand. I love the lightness and almost conversational style she has of writing.

EYE: What is key for you as a reporter?

CARLOTTA: The most important thing is being there, bearing witness, reporting it as it is. I am not a columnist or a great theorist. I'm a basic daily reporter. When I put it together in a book, I try to give it more sense. As you can see, the book is still full of the basic reporting of *"I was there. This is what I saw. This is real. That's how it was."*

The war is what you see happening on the ground, which is incredibly important to report, so that people back home, leaders, families back home know what's happening.

> **There's a great thirst to know what it's like. I see that in readers' reactions to my stories. I know it's a very important job we are doing.**

EYE: Thank you, Carlotta. Your courageous, insightful writing is an inspiration for readers and aspiring reporters alike. Continued success as you embark on your latest assignment in Tunisia as the *New York Times'* North African Bureau Chief.

First published in May, 2014.

Dionne Searcey

New York Times Journalist Dionne Searcey on Her Pursuit of Disobedient Women in West Africa

By Patricia Caso

Dionne Searcey, the award-winning *New York Times* journalist, wrote the unforgettable 2017 *New York Times* article about Boko Haram girls who were trained to be suicide bombers.

> "I saw women who had been strapped with suicide bombs who refused to carry out terrorists' orders in northeastern Nigeria... These women were young and powerless and refused to kill anyone. It was really shocking that they had the bravery to fight one of the most dangerous terrorist groups in the world."
> — *Dionne Searcey*

Dionne now has a memoir, *In Pursuit of Disobedient Women*, which includes that story and gives us a behind-the-scenes look at what it's like to be a correspondent in a foreign country.

This memoir's twist examines what it took to be a mother, wife, breadwinner and journalist as the *Times'* West Africa Bureau Chief from 2015 to 2019. I was intrigued with finding out more from Dionne about her theme of disobedience.

But before delving into her story, I asked about the current global issue, COVID-19...

EYE: What kind of stories are you pursuing with this pandemic now that you and your family are back living in Brooklyn, NY?

DIONNE: Right now I am assigned to the *New York Times'* Politics Desk. What I've been doing is features on political divisions in America. So what I'm looking at is how the virus is exacerbating, or not, that division.

> **I'm really interested in how the pandemic is going to shape our lives, what it's doing to families and to communities, and how it's going to shape our political opinions.**

I think it's really fascinating what lessons we'll learn from this and how we'll go forward.

EYE: How are you handling the pandemic personally?

DIONNE: My husband and I are both working equally while at home, and take turns making dinner or wrangling the kids when one of us has an important call.

Like most people, we've learned to accept the low background hum of kids fighting or complaining and the dog barking in our virtual meetings and calls. Everyone is in the same boat right now.

EYE: What possessed you to up and leave New York five years ago and take the opportunity to be the West Africa Bureau Chief?

DIONNE: I'd always wanted to work abroad, and I really didn't want to move out of New York City to the suburbs, which my husband was pressuring us to do.

We were in a rut in our family life, and it seemed like a way to really shake things up, albeit a dramatic one for most people.

EYE: You titled your memoir *In Pursuit of Disobedient Women*. Would you define "disobedient"?

DIONNE: In this context, I was looking at women who literally defied orders of men in wartime, women who defied expectations of a patriarchal society and women who were some of the most invisible members of societies that are run by governments and boardrooms and even their families.

> They're not decision-makers, they're not leaders of their families, and I wanted to see how they were upending societal expectations and disobeying what was expected of them.

EYE: Can "disobedient" apply to you in any way?

DIONNE: I suppose that by being the main breadwinner while in West Africa I certainly upended expectations in a context where that was not the case for many local women or the majority of other Westerners who lived there.

> I'm well aware of my privilege, however, and could never compare myself to the brave women I met who defied the societal expectations in so many clever ways.

EYE: Is there a particular story or a person who most exemplifies your "disobedient" woman?

DIONNE: I really was taken by one particular young woman in her early 20s named Zalika. She met her husband at a wedding as a teenager and married. She was in tailoring school, sewing school.

Her husband said, "Oh, you don't need to pay for the classes, I'll teach you how to sew." He was a tailor like she wanted to be. She went along with it, dropped out of school, got married and left her family compound.

Then he said basically, "Sorry, you're not going to work. I'm the one who provides."

And she was all by herself all day long. She was sick of it. She did not get to sew. One day she got sick and sent him out for medicine. He came back at the end of the day and forgotten to bring the medicine. I think anyone who is married or has a longtime partner can relate to that exasperation.

> **Also, she had often noticed when they did go out together, he was looking at other women. And she was really sick of it. What was amazing about this situation is she went to an Iman to get divorced. He wasn't cheating on her, abusing her or hurting her in any way. But what she wanted was love.**

And that was a new thing for women in this part of the world, where girls are uneducated and are forcibly married. Young women don't often have their own careers, and their needs aren't respected.

EYE: What was the most dangerous situation you witnessed in West Africa??

DIONNE: I saw women who had been strapped with suicide bombs who refused to carry out terrorists' orders in northeastern Nigeria where Boko Haram, an Islamic extremist group, was operating.

These women were young and powerless and refused to kill anyone. It was really shocking that they had the bravery to fight one of the most dangerous terrorist groups in the world.

EYE: That must have been terrifying to cover. Is there a story that has had an international impact?

DIONNE: I reported about a civilian massacre and interviewed many people again in northeastern Nigeria where the military had rolled into town and accused everyone of supporting Boko Haram or being Boko Haram members.

> **The military lined up all the men and opened fire on all of them and then went on to a neighboring village. I met with one man who had been shot several times, but somehow miraculously managed to survive.**

Then I talked with other women who had seen what happened to their husbands. I think that story rattled the Nigerian government, and the U.N. wound up not including Nigeria on the Human Rights Commission. I was proud that the story got a lot of attention.

EYE: You have worked in very dangerous areas. Was there a craziest moment in any of your international reporting?

DIONNE: There were so many crazy moments. One was when I was in Syria riding in the back of a car and my fixer, a local journalist and friend, got a phone call. He just listened for a while and hung up.

He said, "I think you'd better leave right now. Some sort of state security service, like the secret police, is warning me about you." *What does that mean?* I wondered. He turned around and said, "They're not going to shoot you, but will probably shoot at you."

So I decided that maybe it was time that I get out of town, and we left.

EYE: How do you get the people you interview in these very tense and horrible situations to trust you?

DIONNE: A lot of reporters forget to channel their own empathy. It is a very important reporting tool to understand your reactions as a human being and use that in your reporting. Empathy can really help you ask good questions, which can help people open up to you.

> Also, a lot of people whom I talked with understood my role as a journalist and that I was a vehicle to get some help. These people had insanely traumatic experiences and no one had ever bothered to ask what happened.

A lot of them hadn't even told their moms or their husbands or anyone else what had happened. They understood I could be a messenger to get the word out and maybe someone could help or just offer understanding of what they were going through.

EYE: What do you hope comes from writing this memoir?

DIONNE: We had hoped by my own experiences as a wife and mother that people could understand that regular people can move to places we don't often think about. But what I wanted to convey the most was that Americans should be more focused on the African continent.

So many are so fixated on Europe or Asia. In these African countries, leaders are doing amazing work. This is a place that has a vibrant, rich, exciting culture—these stories deserve to be listened to and acted upon.

EYE: What is it about journalism that intrigued you as a career when you started as a crime reporter at the City News Bureau of Chicago?

DIONNE: I really love journalism. Where else can you immerse yourself in one topic and learn everything you can about it in a short amount of time and then move on to something else?

I've had this range of beats where I've covered everything from local government to courts to police reporting to state government and politics.

> I did a couple stints in Iraq during the war. I've covered earthquakes. It's such a privilege to be on the inside of things, talk to interesting people and then to get to explain what is going on.

I love to be able to shape the story, to think of a new idea, to have people listen to me and to be that kind of conduit that helps people understand what's going on in the world.

EYE: I was intrigued with the idea that you like to balance each tough story you do with a hopeful one.

DIONNE: That was pretty much a direct response to criticism of Western reporters who go to the African continent and only write about famine and disease and war and malnutrition and all the bad things.

> When you're a *New York Times* reporter, presidents read your work, the State Department reads your work, the UN and so on. You can be a voice for the bad things going on maybe more than any other publication in the world.

I wanted to be hyper-aware that I didn't portray only violence. All these countries have poets, painters, art galleries and fancy restaurants. The horrible war with Boko Haram is confined to a very small part of the country. I thought it was important to balance things out.

EYE: You became the breadwinner, your husband had taken on less responsibility for his job and you had your three young kids with you in West Africa. How did you ultimately handle all of that?

DIONNE: Going running. Not like a fast runner or a far runner, though. I really like that headspace where you can just go out and be by yourself. I think when you're a parent and you work and you're in a relationship, you just need a little bit of time by yourself to think things through and to recharge a little bit.

> **Open communication with everybody in the family, including the kids, is really important, as is staying in touch with colleagues through WhatsApp groups. Those were lifelines.**

EYE: What strengths do you personally count on for your successful writing, investigating and interviewing?

DIONNE: I like to pick out stories that can have resonance. In West Africa, it was writing about social issues, about how women were treated or what was expected of wives or even migration, how young men were often victims of migration. And no one really focused on that, even though these people were part of families and breadwinners.

I don't always get it right. But when you do, that's a really nice feeling.

EYE: Thank you, Dionne, for your generous time and dedication to journalism. We look forward to reading more of your important reporting.

First published in April, 2020.

Elaine Weiss

The Woman's Hour Author Elaine Weiss on the Dramatic Battle for the Right to Vote

By Stacey Gualandi

I am so lucky to be able to speak with author Elaine Weiss, an award-winning journalist who has written a new book, *The Woman's Hour: The Great Fight to Win the Vote.*

> "I think this story needs to be brought to our population. That's what I wanted to do. I just hope it'll inspire women to know more about their history, their legacy and to act on it and not be passive."
>
> —*Elaine Weiss*

It's a fascinating and painstakingly detailed look at a pivotal, six-week period back in 1920 when a group of audacious activists just barely secured the right for women to vote. I caught up with Elaine at her home in Baltimore, sitting at the very desk where she wrote the book…

EYE: Was this whole story of how women got the vote something you were always fascinated by, or did it just fall into your lap?

ELAINE: A little bit of both. I had written a book about women in World War I who had organized themselves and taken on roles that women had never done before—in industries, agriculture and science.

> I was struck that a lot of these women were suffragists who were trying to prove to the United States government that they were patriotic, that they were citizens and that they deserved the vote. That was an interesting aspect of my research for that book.

Then I was researching another topic about a woman who had made a bequest to the suffragists in 1914. I was reading about where that money went. I trained as a journalist, so I was chasing the money and was fascinated by how that bequest, which was very large at the time—two million dollars, which would be more than 50 million dollars today—was spent.

I found that it was spent in public relations, on a press office for the suffragists, on a lobbying infrastructure in Washington, and to lobby for the 19th Amendment, the Federal Women's Suffrage Amendment, as it was nearing the passage in Congress.

Then part of it went to establish the League of Women Voters and part went towards the ratification campaign, because even after Congress passed the 19th Amendment, it had been stranded there in willful neglect for 40 years.

EYE: So it took a long time!

ELAINE: Forty years! It finally made its way out of Congress by the thinnest of margins. We tend to think that everyone was on board and excited about women voting, but that's not true. Then it had to go to the states—there were 48 at that time.

> Three quarters of the states have to ratify any new amendment to the Constitution, and so they needed 36 states. What happened with the last state to ratify was an amazing story that I read in a report in the Library of Congress.

EYE: Is that what started you thinking you had a book to write?

ELAINE: I was thinking *Wow, this is really a dramatic story.* Then as I researched it more deeply, I realized that contained in that dramatic six weeks were all the themes, all the arguments and all the political pressures that characterized the entire fight for women's suffrage, and you had a lot of the characters who reached back in history.

By telling the front story and then doing flashbacks into the origins of the moment and how they progressed, I saw there was a much richer story than just one dramatic element.

EYE: How long did it take you to do all this research? When did you start working on it?

ELAINE: In the summer of 2013. I researched and wrote the book in about three-and-a-quarter years. That is pretty efficient for a book of that size, and then of course there's production and editing—add some time for that. So I started five years ago, but I handed it in during the fall of 2016.

EYE: But you, singlehandedly, have brought these people to life—the suffragists, the women who were against enfranchising women to get the vote, the politicians, the journalists of the time. Did you feel like you got to know them as if they were your friends?

ELAINE: Thank you. I tried very hard. I think one of the most surprising things I've learned is that I thought I was the only one who had not been taught this completely in high school or college or grad school, but I'm finding most people say, "I never learned that. I never knew that."

Women's suffrage is usually dismissed in about one sentence between the Progressive Era and the Roaring '20s, and that's it.

EYE: Yes, we know the names Susan B. Anthony and even Elizabeth Cady Stanton, but it's the Carrie Catts, the Sue Whites, these people who were at the forefront of the suffrage movement, whom we get to know through you.

ELAINE: I guess the remarkable thing about the movement is that it has to be carried on by three generations of women. Three generations, and they very carefully teach, mentor and cultivate the next generation who are going to take on the tasks. I find that interesting and inspiring and something we should be looking at. It was a very conscious decision to bring up the next generation of leaders.

So, we're now in the third generation when my story takes place in the summer of 1920, and I wanted these women and the men in the story to be real people and to have foibles and vanities and to be nervous about things, which I could tell they were because I was reading their letters and their memos and their secret notes to allies.

> That gave me insight into who they, especially the women, were; in this third generation there are these incredibly talented and dedicated citizen activists.

EYE: As you have said, this was a long, bitter fight. It was three generations of women. It took more than 70 years to get to that point, which is completely shocking. There were so many people against this. It took a huge societal shift to make this happen.

ELAINE: Right. It's not just a political question. The women's suffrage question really is, as I describe it, a precursor to what we call the culture wars. It's very much a social, societal, cultural, domestic and personal debate about women's role in society and in the home.

So it has all of these passions swirling around it that a simple political decision would not. It becomes very, very complicated.

> You have advocacy and opposition in surprising places, including a well organized group of women who oppose giving their sisters the vote.

EYE: What was it about these women that made them so determined to do this? They were mocked and ridiculed. I imagine their lives could have been in danger.

ELAINE: Yes, they were threatened all the time. First, they believed that this was an injustice, that half of the nation had no voice in their own government. Twenty-seven million women would be eligible to vote. Of course, there were more women than that.

What's so fascinating to me is even in 1920 it's ridiculed as maybe not preposterous but unwise. Of course we hear echoes of that today—which was really stunning to me as I wrote the last sections of the book during the 2016 presidential election.

EYE: Here we are 100 years later and has anything changed? It's gotten better obviously.

ELAINE: Yes, women are able to vote, but I think we need to realize that even the 19th Amendment allowing half of the citizens to have a voice, was also not the mark of perfection because black women in the south were still not allowed to vote.

> **They had it on paper in the Constitution, but in practice they were intimidated and forced not to vote.**

EYE: You're shining big pulsating arrows on voting issues. I see that it's been very well reviewed, and even the *New York Times* said something about getting goosebumps reading about the lead-up to that final moment when it came down to Tennessee, as you said, in Nashville.

This was the state that was going to put it over the edge. What was it that finally got them over that last hump to get the right to vote?

ELAINE: Actually, one of the things I get great pleasure from is readers telling me they did get goose-bumps and they really were worried, in those last sections of the book, about whether it was going to happen.

What's sobering is that it almost doesn't happen. It's not like everyone in the nation stands up and says, "Oh, yes, this is right. How silly that women are not given the opportunity to have a voice in who represents them. How silly it is that they're not allowed to sit on juries."

> That is depending on the state. The 19th Amendment did open the door for women to be on juries, but it depended on the state and whether they implemented that, and some of them didn't implement it for another 20, 30, 40 years.

EYE: Yes, there were 12 states that flat-out said either no or they weren't going to get involved in this at all. So how close did the amendment come to not being ratified?

ELAINE: It was very close to defeat. I'm not saying it wouldn't have passed eventually, but I think that the reason this fight in Tennessee in the summer of 1920 was so bitter and so dramatic is because everyone realized this may be the last stand.

The suffragists see that momentum has been working against them all through the spring and early summer of 1920. There have been only rejections, and the anti-suffragists are getting more determined and throwing more money into the campaigns against ratification, and getting more sinister in their maneuvers pressuring the presidential candidates.

It unfolds during a presidential campaign, making the whole process more intense. And they see that the country is really swinging into a more reactionary mode, more isolated, more nativist, more conservative.

They're afraid that if they're not able to tap this last moment, they really may have to wait a long time to be able to get this amendment through.

EYE: It sounds very intense.

ELAINE: Yes, for them and for the anti-suffragists; they're on a roll. They've managed to have even Delaware, which isn't really a southern state, not ratified. And it gets close in New Jersey. And in Maryland where I live, it got rejected. There are pockets of resistance in odd places.

EYE: One thing that boggles my mind is that there was a whole movement of women saying, "No, we shouldn't have this right. We shouldn't be enfranchised." That's what I just don't understand.

ELAINE: They don't see it as in their best interest. They're going to enter into the world of dirty politics; they're going to be degraded by it. Of course, they say it will also destroy the American home because women, once they get the right to vote, are going to abandon their families.

They also fear that women will work outside the home, and, of course, that doesn't happen immediately because there's such resistance, but it begins to happen. Every working woman I know has had a version of that even now. "Shouldn't you be home with your kids? What are you sacrificing for your career?"

> So what I hope is that people read the book, eventually see the film adaptation, and say, "Wow, people fought. People were imprisoned. People suffered. People believed that this nation is a democracy.

It is *We the people*, and the greatest gift of a democracy is the ability to vote." How can you be blasé about that? I truly don't understand.

EYE: The thing that made me sad is that the women who were at the forefront of this movement never got to see it ratified. Also, I read at the end in your acknowledgements about how your mom and one of your best friends didn't get to see your book. Is that hard?

ELAINE: Yes. My mom died just before I began, and my friend died just as I ended the book. And then another friend died just as it came out. This is life, and it's the will of life. It's bittersweet, but I think they would be very pleased by the reception and by people thinking and believing this is an important story, a story that was not brought to the forefront until now.

EYE: Exactly! Thank you so much for your time. Again, the book is called *The Woman's Hour: The Great Fight to Win the Vote*. Binge the book, and I understand there may be at TV series that could be binged when it comes out. Thank you, Elaine. I really appreciate you talking to us.

First published in August, 2018.

Fernanda Santos

Journalist Fernanda Santos on Covering One of the Deadliest Days in American Firefighting from the Human Angle

By Catherine Anaya

Meet Fernanda Santos, a journalist who prides herself in telling true stories, who has reported in three languages, speaks four and is learning a fifth. She got her start in Rio de Janeiro and is now Phoenix Bureau Chief for the *New York Times*.

> "There is always an interesting human angle to everything we cover. And those to me are the stories that are most memorable... those are the stories that get people to care and want to change things."
>
> —*Fernanda Santos*

Fernanda has covered almost every subject imaginable, and now she has written her first book, *The Fireline: The Story of the Granite Mountain Hot Shots and One of the Deadliest Days in American Firefighting*. Here to talk with us about reporting and much more is Fernanda Santos...

EYE: You cover New Mexico in addition to Arizona. That's a big territory. I want to talk a little bit about your background before we get into the book. You were based in New York prior to coming to Phoenix. Was the transition from New York to sunny Arizona difficult for you?

FERNANDA: No, not at all, and the reason is that I am from Brazil originally; I guess once you leave your home country, every place is different and no place is like home truly.

I grew up with a very big family, a very warm family. I lived with my parents up until the moment I came here. I was 25 when I came to this country. So coming to Phoenix was an adventure for me.

I had been in New York for 11 years. I was in Massachusetts before that for a few years. And I was very interested in learning about different parts of this country. I felt that being in New York, I was in this bubble. My husband and our daughter, who was three at the time, were really excited about coming here.

EYE: You came to the U.S. in 1998. What brought you here?

FERNANDA: I came to go to graduate school. I was a reporter in Rio. And as is common with reporters, I covered a lot of breaking news stories. There's a lot of that in Rio and a lot that you cover that doesn't ever make it into the paper because, sadly, violence is a fact of daily life there.

> **I slowly begin to realize that when I went out with my friends, I had very little talk about other than really sad, horrible things. So I became very interested in trying to carve a new path. For me, it was never my intention to stay here.**

But I applied for graduate school and got accepted at Boston University and a couple of other places. I chose Boston because I had never been there. One thing led to another, and I am still here 17 years later.

EYE: Going back to your time in Rio, I've read that the violence that you witnessed and experienced was a catalyst for you wanting to become a journalist. Tell me about that.

FERNANDA: I've always been very interested in the human side of every story. I remember very vividly when we moved to Rio from Salvador, which is the capital of the state on the north-northeastern part of Brazil, to this beautiful apartment that had a view of the mountains where there was a slum, the largest slum in South America.

I could see the houses coming to the side of the mountain we lived in. I was always interested in who were those people living there. I was about 12 or 13 years old. There was this one moment when there was a huge rainstorm. We have very heavy rains in March. And I watched from my house these houses being washed away by the rain.

EYE: And then what further grabbed your attention to the story?

FERNANDA: I saw a little thing about it in the paper the next day. I became obsessed from that moment on with finding out the stories behind the stories. Who are these people? How can we devote just a few paragraphs in the newspaper?

> **These people lost everything they had. They died. I became very curious about them. Every act of violence or natural catastrophe that I witnessed in Rio or wherever I went made me want to know about the people.**

I think ultimately the greatest driving force for me was that behind every person who pulls a trigger and behind everybody who gets shot there is a very complicated life—and many times a very interesting story. That's what humanizes journalism.

That's what I strive to do. Those are the stories that get people talking. How could this have happened? What can we do to prevent it from happening again?

EYE: The pinnacle of your career in journalism is now being bureau chief. What do you think distinguishes you in a very competitive and grueling profession?

FERNANDA: I didn't grow up in this country, so even though I've been here all these years, I still look at things in a way a lot of people here don't. Sometimes it doesn't help me, because my editors can't quite understand how this could be an angle for a story or how this could even be a story.

Other times I'm covering exactly the same thing everybody else is covering, but I am bringing a perspective they're not seeing, because either it's so common to them that they can't notice it anymore or because it's so weird that they wouldn't even think about it.

I think also that I really love to talk. And, I really love to listen. Journalism is really a listening profession. We are almost like therapists sometimes to people. I'm sure you've been many times in situations where people are crying and you're crying with them. And by the way, don't think there's anything wrong with that.

EYE: You've traveled all over the world. What has been the most impactful story for you personally, and why?

FERNANDA: Obviously, the Yarnell fire was incredibly moving for me, to the point that I became somewhat obsessed with it. And my husband one day said, *You know, you should just write a book.* I really wasn't thinking about this as a book from the start.

> **But I can see in my head right now all these other stories that maybe didn't mean a lot, maybe didn't make a big splash in the paper, weren't even front-page stories, but stories that I never really forgot.**

One I always think about is, you know it's silly, but it's about a dog in New Mexico. He was an 11-year-old Australian blue dog. He has since died. But at the time, this town had passed an ordinance that would require all dogs to be leashed because in a nearby town, a woman had been mauled to death by a pit bull. This was a stray dog.

But it gave me hope that we still have that fire inside us, because half the town was petitioning for this dog to be leashed and the other half wanted the dog to roam free.

It became a big deal in town. They had a hearing and there was an overflow crowd. They put speakers in the parking lot. And in the end, they came up with a compromise. And Blue was allowed to stay in this area within a wireless fence.

> When we sit down and discuss our differences with civility, we're able to come to a point where everybody's sort of happy with things—it's a small, small thing. But I said that if that could be done in this place, why not in every other place, right on this planet?

EYE: You mentioned people coming together for one issue. I think of that in 2013 with the Yarnell Fire, the loss of 19 men. I don't think I've ever seen Arizona come together quite like we did at that point. And you said you became so obsessed by it that you wrote this book. Why did you feel the need to write a book?

FERNANDA: I knew that space to be devoted to stories about this fire would be limited, and would come to an end at some point. I wrote several stories. I did a big Sunday piece exploring what may have gone wrong, but I still had a lot of very basic questions about fires.

And I could tell from the very beginning, having covered the FDNY in New York when I worked there, having covered numerous funerals after 9/11, that firefighters don't make decisions that are predicated on the possibility of somebody losing their lives.

They take a lot of risks, but they don't take foolish risks. I wanted to understand what kind of men those 19 Granite Mountain Hotshots were to have taken on that decision to go into a place the fire hadn't burned, which is more likely to burn, and also to have made a decision to stay together.

EYE: You say it was important for you to find out who these firefighters were.

FERNANDA: The 19 men were found within a space of 20 by 30 feet, very close together, side by side in many cases. I started to think, why would I ever do that if I saw that death was imminent? Why wouldn't I try to run, and die trying at least? You know, I have a husband; I have a daughter. And they all had somebody who was very meaningful to them.

> **Three of them had pregnant wives at home. Their kids were all little. So they had reasons to live. Yet they chose to stay together. That's ultimately the question I wanted to answer. And to answer that question, I had to understand who they were.**

EYE: The book is called *The Fireline*. You mentioned something very important: that this book is not about what went wrong. It's about who these men were and why they stayed together.

You took an eight-month unpaid leave of absence from the *Times* to write this book. You interviewed families, best friends, colleagues for all 19 men. Were you surprised that so many were willing to talk to you and that there were a few who were so reluctant?

FERNANDA: I was not surprised that they were reluctant or that people wanted to talk. What was difficult for some of them to understand is that the interviews I wanted to have with them were not the typical interviews they'd had right after the fire happened.

Those people had never talked to reporters before. And all of a sudden they were inundated with requests for interviews. Cameras at their doors and so forth. I told them *I want to talk to you with time. I really want to understand about your husband or your son. And you are the person who's going to introduce him to me.* That takes time.

EYE: How did you manage to talk to everybody?

FERNANDA: I made a decision that I was not going to knock on people's doors, because I knew they were just so fed up with it. So I worked with what I call a buddy system.

I knew one of the widows whom I had talked with as I was reporting for the *Times* on the fire. I asked her to approach somebody else and somebody else. And then, little by little, I got to talk to everybody.

I wrote letters to nine families whom I couldn't reach, and three got back to me. And then at one point I had talked with all of them. I think the biggest surprise was actually that they all wanted to talk.

EYE: Fernanda's book is a compelling read; I highly recommend it. Thank you so much for talking with me, Fernanda. I really appreciate it.

First published in December, 2016.

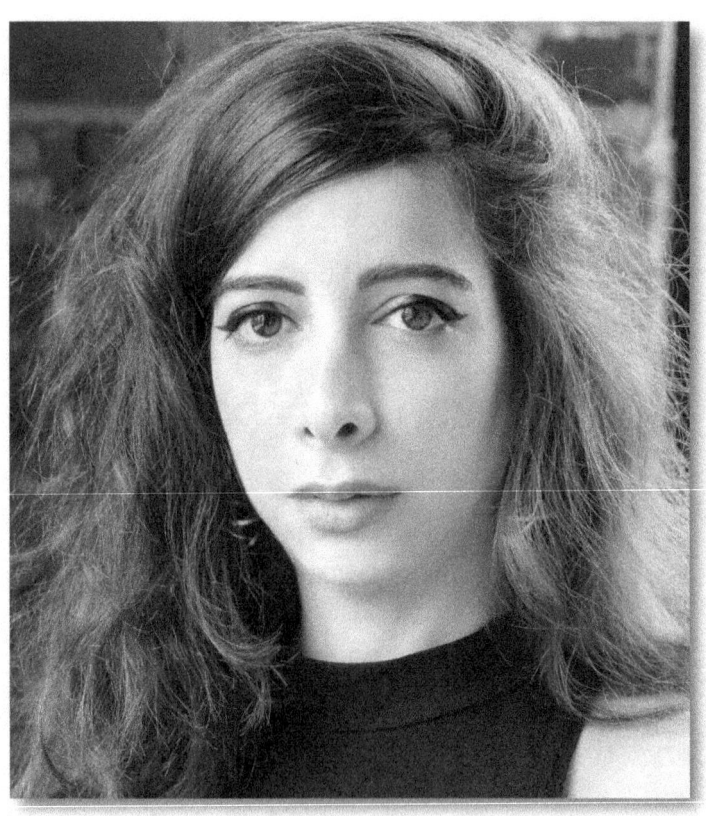

Zahra Hankir

Journalist Zahra Hankir Spotlights Arab Women Reporters in Their Own Words

By Patricia Caso

London-based journalist Zahra Hankir has covered Middle East and Arab political turmoil and violence throughout her career, but admittedly not to the detriment of her safety. She was well aware that many women journalists, who live in and report from those diverse regions, face unbelievable odds to get the truth out. Zahra was shocked to notice they received little credit. She stepped up to change that.

> "I was fascinated by information-gathering and dissemination, and the idea that the pursuit of truth and its reflection could be a profession. My obsession with journalism and the Arab world persisted over the years, and it culminated in this book."
> *—Zahra Hankir*

In *Our Women on the Ground—Essays by Arab Women Reporting from the Arab World*, Zahra asked 19 courageous reporters to share their powerful, unvarnished perspectives on their jobs and lives. Zahra took time to describe the importance of these journalists, known as sahafiya...

EYE: What is your goal in highlighting Arab and Middle Eastern women journalists?

ZAHRA: To give Arab women reporters a global platform so they can share their experiences of reporting from and living in the region from which they hail.

> **The Arab world and its people are so often seen as homogeneous, when the geographic area is intricately layered, and each woman and country and conflict carries unique truths.**

This is also a long-overdue act of celebration and appreciation for the incredible work these women have been doing on the ground over the decades, amidst seismic societal shifts and widespread displacement triggered by violent warfare and its crippling aftermath.

EYE: How dangerous is the work?

ZAHRA: Local Arab women often risk their lives at the front lines as they cover their home or neighboring countries, and they haven't historically been celebrated in this way and in these spaces. These women are not war correspondents or foreign reporters.

These journalists, correspondents and photographers are natives who tell different, more personal stories about conflict and its devastating consequences on their own people.

The women face steep and unique challenges that their Western counterparts do not. With all that in mind, their stories can't help but be fascinating, and their work must be celebrated.

EYE: Why did you decide to compile their stories through personal essays and not interviews?

ZAHRA: I wanted the women in this book to tell their stories sans filters, and without any specific audience in mind, Western or otherwise. I acted as a guide, when I was needed, and I did indeed edit and curate the book and make editorial suggestions along the way.

I ultimately hoped they would tell whatever story felt most poignant to them, and wanted them to be ready to tell that story. Looking at how the essays turned out—their range; the raw, intimate details they contain; and the honesty with which they were written—I believe this was the right approach.

EYE: Were you surprised by any of the essays?

ZAHRA: It's not that I didn't expect the women to write openly and honestly, but I was, on occasion, knocked sideways by the extent to which they used their pens to excavate previously unearthed feelings.

> **I was in constant awe of their bravery, and their willingness to push boundaries without even intending to do so.**

Zaina Erhaim, a Syrian journalist, for example, writes about how she had become so desensitized to violence in her hometown that one day, as she wiped blood off her car following a bombing at a nearby school, she called her friend and casually asked her what they should have for lunch that day.

Nada Bakri, a former journalist from Lebanon, wrote for the first time about the grief she endured after she lost her husband, Anthony Shadid, during the Arab Spring—there is no resolution in that chapter, no happy ending, no hopeful thread. The end of the essay is a gut punch.

EYE: Why did you choose this format?

ZAHRA: It doesn't follow what a traditional essay might look like. Indeed, this book does not sugarcoat. In many ways it reflects the situation in the Arab world today—resilience against a very real backdrop of tragedy and hopelessness.

I was also surprised by the extent to which I was emotionally invested in the book and the women's stories.

I constantly felt guilty that I wasn't doing enough, that I was living in privilege, editing these essays from the comfort of my home in North London while these women and millions of others in the region struggle with harrowing daily realities.

EYE: What did you find drives these women to continually face up to the sexism, violence, etc.?

ZAHRA: I would note it's the desire to share and disseminate the truth that drives several of the women in the book. They have a profound understanding of how and why women are treated in the way that they are in their respective societies, and they fight misogyny by breaking into spaces they may not be welcome or expected in.

EYE: Is there a pattern among these women journalists in what they want to achieve and how they do it?

ZAHRA: The women were all unflinchingly committed to the act of journalism and the art of newsgathering. Their tenacity, resourcefulness and resilience jump off the pages.

Perhaps this tenacity is best captured and expressed by Sudanese journalist and columnist Shamael el Noor, who never once doubts or reconsiders her career path, despite enduring grave challenges and constant threats to her safety.

She speaks poetically of journalism, not only as a profession, but as a way of life:

> "I didn't fully understand the value of my choices until after I faced all this danger and harassment—from the state, from tribesmen, and from Islamists. I have been a journalist for a decade now, and let me tell you what I have learned: this is what journalism should be, or else it shouldn't be, at all.
>
> Though these experiences have had high prices, they haven't weakened or deterred me. I have no other option but to move forward, like the many brave journalists who face persecution. This is our destiny, and we remain ever devoted to it."

EYE: Are there people or places these women can access that their male counterparts cannot?

ZAHRA: Women-dominated spaces and women-focused stories. For example, Amira Al-Sharif, a Yemeni photojournalist, enters the private homes of Yemeni women whose husbands and sons were lost to or engaged in war, to tell us stories of their strength and resilience.

Heba Shibani, a Libyan broadcast journalist, turns her attention to women's rights by hosting a show that tackled major issues including the inability of Libyan women to pass their nationality on to their children.

EYE: CNN's chief international anchor Christiane Amanpour said these women journalists "live and work in unrest and oppression." How do they become journalists to begin with?

ZAHRA: These women were resourceful in overcoming many challenges, including having to contend with families that opposed their career choices, sexist and misogynist workplaces, and threats of detention and arrest by the state.

In some cases they persisted with their ambitions behind their parents' backs. Amira Al-Sharif snuck into local souks to take photos of Yemenis and documented university protests behind her father's back.

She eventually won her family's trust by persuading them, through her work, that this was a noble and necessary profession, and indeed the only one she wanted to pursue.

Egyptian journalist Eman Helal hid her bloodied clothing from her family after covering the fallout from the uprisings in Egypt. And she fought against the patriarchy by using her camera as a tool against sexual harassers. These are just two in a sea of examples.

EYE: What was your biggest challenge in editing this anthology?

ZAHRA: Ensuring an accurate portrayal of the region by diversifying the contributors to the best of my ability. Given space constraints, and the fact that we were dealing with a region containing 22 countries with more than 400 million people, it was a somewhat impossible task to begin with.

I also wanted to include a range of time periods to give readers a broader perspective on political and social history, rather than just the Arab Spring.

> **While I'm pleased with how the book has turned out, I understand there are stories and conflicts and countries that were excluded. This is something I definitely lost sleep over, even though in some ways it was out of my control.**

EYE: Did you always want a journalism career from a young age?

ZAHRA: Yes! I grew up in the United Kingdom, where I was born to Lebanese parents who had left the country during a drawn-out and devastating civil war. My parents constantly watched the news to follow up on what was unraveling in their—our—home country.

Landlines were frequently down, so they weren't able to regularly speak to their families to stay abreast of the dire situation.

So I grew up thinking of journalists as heroes, portals into another world who had the power to disseminate otherwise inaccessible information and who could shed light on faraway lands and complicated conflicts.

EYE: What do you look for in a story before you commit to it?

ZAHRA: Tension, growth and/or change.

EYE: What do you want the reader to take away from these essays?

ZAHRA: I hope readers will come away from *Our Women on the Ground* with a deeper and more nuanced understanding of the Middle East. Also, that they will look more closely at who's telling the stories of its countries and people, and seek out more diverse and specifically women's voices.

Ultimately I hope readers will recognize the work these women are doing as crucial to our full understanding of the Arab world, and celebrate them.

EYE: Finally, what is next for you?

ZAHRA: While more and more Arab women are being heard in this space, and more newsrooms are employing and supporting locals, there's much more to be done.

I'm passionate about amplifying the voices of Arab women and Arabs in general, and in advocating for more diverse newsrooms and more inclusive narratives, so I hope to embark on another project in this area. I'm not yet sure what format it will take.

EYE: Thank you, Zahra, for your time and for your introductions to these journalists who are bringing real events of the Arab and Middle Eastern countries to the world. Continued success to you!

First published in September, 2019.

Part IV
Broadcasters:
Using Their Voices

"I believe that good journalism, good television, can make our world a better place."

—*Christiane Amanpour,* Journalist and Television Host

Clarissa Ward

International Correspondent Clarissa Ward Witnesses History *On All Fronts*

By *Stacey Gualandi*

From Beirut to Beijing to Baghdad, Clarissa Ward, CNN's Chief International Correspondent, reports from front lines around the world. As a conflict reporter for the past 15 years, she has earned multiple Emmy, Murrow, and Peabody Awards.

> "My part is shining a light on spots in the world and telling people's stories who maybe wouldn't have an opportunity to tell them otherwise."
>
> —*Clarissa Ward*

Where there's a crisis, there's Clarissa. But it is the untold stories that inspired her new book, *On All Fronts: The Education of a Journalist*. I'm excited to be able to chat with her...

EYE: You're in London and you have two-month-old Casper and a two-year-old son, Ezra. After reading the book, I know that you completely understand sleep deprivation, but is it different when you have two children?

CLARISSA: It is. Now I look back and I think, *Wow, one kid was really a walk in the park, but two kids is like a trek through the jungle in the Congo.* But yes, trying to juggle it all—and now with this new normal of working from home—is tough. My kids are in the basement right now, with people caring for them while we talk.

EYE: I read that if not for 9/11, you might never have found your calling. Somebody asked you in your book, "What's the juice for you?" Was that the initial juice?

CLARISSA: I think for every American, 9/11 was like a thunderbolt from the sky. Your world was turned upside down and it never really went back to normal. You find a new normal, but it's different than the old normal. I'm always struck by that when I meet young people who are born after that.

> **It was almost immediate. I felt like I needed to be more engaged with the world. I needed to go out and understand what the hell is going on, why these people wanted to kill us, why we have been misunderstood—or have we been misunderstood—have we done something to precipitate this, what is our role in this?**

These are all questions I found myself asking, and I felt compelled to go and start telling these stories. I wanted to tell them in a way where there was a human element, because it's so easy when you get into the geopolitical jargon and you're talking about things, to lose sight of the fact that you're talking about lives, you're talking about people.

> Of course, I was 21 years old at the time. You learn a lot along the way, and you realize that you can't change the world and then, later on, you make peace with the fact that you're not actually supposed to change the world. You're supposed to just do your part.

EYE: Speaking of that, so many of the stories of these people that you met along the way were about drivers, tutors and fixers. How important is it for you to tell stories of those people?

CLARISSA: It's so important because when you watch my stories on the evening news, you're only getting half the picture. You're seeing this is what's going on, this is who's fighting whom, this is what happened today, and occasionally you'll get a feel for suffering and war and the drama and sadness and the horror.

But what you don't get a feel for are the much more subtle interactions going on behind the camera, the small acts of kindness from countless people, the moments of tears, the acts of cruelty, the moments of hilarity.

These small things, the conversations with drivers, the small moments that of course don't make it to the evening news—they are actually what inform and shape a journalist's opinion and understanding of a story, a people and a place.

> **Because they don't make it to the evening news, I do feel it's important that they make it somewhere. Their stories need to be told because it comes back to that humanizing effect, again, that I was talking about.**

EYE: I felt like I was there with you, especially in Chapter 8. That just gutted me because it was all about covering what was happening in Syria and witnessing loss of life—people who were literally so close to you. I don't know how you can compartmentalize that.

CLARISSA: You can't take it all in because then you are not able to function any longer. I started to find that with Syria. It was becoming an unsustainable level of taking it in as much as I wanted to. But I do think it's this blessing and this curse, this constant push and pull, because the better my work was in Syria, the more I was involved and immersed. If I tried to pull away, I feel the work was not then at that high standard.

EYE: It must be hard to keep that level of intensity up.

CLARISSA: In order to get the work to that place where it's so compelling, where it's so compassionate, where it's so full and rich, you have to give of yourself emotionally—and that's difficult and it's not always sustainable.

> **I think, as I said, other journalists have different ways of achieving greatness in their work, but for me, I need to be immersed and open to another person's full experience in order for the piece to really make that punching impact.**

EYE: What do you think sets you apart and perhaps has led to so much success in your career?

CLARISSA: I think there's a couple of things. I've always been obsessed with the idea of getting to places other people can't get to. In order to do that kind of work, to interview ISIS fighters, to go and embed with the Taliban, you need to spend an awful lot of time building up trust and relationships with people whom frankly you would not normally choose to go for a coffee with.

I'm being a little glib there, but the point is that a lot of journalists are just understandably not willing to invest that time in characters who are frankly enraging and often deplorable. I have really felt it's important to hear every side of the story and it's important to listen, even if we don't necessarily agree.

> I think the other thing is that the same reason I tried to learn a lot of languages, and I should stress I speak them all at very humble levels, but for me, I really thrive on connection. That is the juice for me. That's what this is all about for me.

That's why I couldn't see myself hosting a show in the studio. I need to be out there, I need to be connecting with people and then, once I connect with them, I can tell you guys, here's what this is about.

EYE: You've put yourself in so many situations that are life-threatening. Are you afraid?

CLARISSA: Absolutely! Honestly, I am really a fearful person. I'm actually a little bit of a chicken. I know that sounds ridiculous. I'm not tough. I freak out when bombs are falling when…well, I don't freak out because you actually *can't* freak out.

If you're a freak-out person, you need to find a different profession. I freak out deep in here, but on the outside, I shut down a bit. I spend so much time trying to ensure that I don't put myself in situations where bullets are whizzing past my head, because I'm not interested in that.

That doesn't do it for me. There are people who are much better at doing that and are much better at commentating on the military side of things, which is not my area of expertise.

EYE: But how do you prepare for reporting in a hot zone?

CLARISSA: I want to be as close to the action as I need to be, to get to where civilians are. Those are the voices I'm usually most interested in hearing in conflict zones. I don't thrive on adrenaline.

I really find it very stressful, so I am very mindful of going to the places I need to go to and trying to get the shot I need to get, but I have no interest in taking any gratuitous risks.

EYE: Talking about risk, you are not someone who's going to say, "I'm done with reporting because I'm now a mom." You're going to keep right on doing what you're doing, but what changes now that you've got two kids?

CLARISSA: I'll tell you what changes. Obviously, you're even more mindful of security because it's not just about you anymore. I now have two people in my life who I love way more than I love myself, which is petrifying, and the bar is high.

I need to come back from this assignment in one piece and I'm very, very mindful of that, but the thing that you don't necessarily plan for is how it will change you emotionally. I remember when I was six or seven months pregnant going to Yemen and I was interviewing this woman. Her son was on the floor between us and he was severely malnourished; he was dying.

> I reached out and touched his hair just like an act of affection, and I felt his warm body under my hand and I just lost it. I totally lost it. I couldn't stop crying because of the horror of the fact that this little boy was dying on the floor and hundreds of thousands of people might know about it through my report, but nothing would change and the world would keep turning. I just was consumed by the agony of it.

EYE: How has it changed your reporting?

CLARISSA: Let's be clear, I'd seen children dying in war zones before; it's always awful. But since becoming a mother, it's like wearing your heart outside of your body. I am so sensitive—so exquisitely tender in a sense to any act of cruelty or suffering in a child—that it's extremely emotional.

What that's done, other than embarrass me on a few occasions because I'm like, "I shouldn't be the one crying when your son is the one who is sick. I'm sorry for that and it's not very professional of me," is to inject more compassion into my reporting. I feel like we need that.

EYE: I imagine it's got to be difficult for you as a journalist because you can't snap your fingers and solve the problem.

CLARISSA: Part of what you need to survive in this industry for a long time is that you need to understand you're riding a wave. Sometimes you're on the story and it's the hot story and you're getting the goods and it's amazing, and sometimes you're on a story and it's a great story, but it just isn't getting the attention that you would like to see it get.

You just have to ride the wave. You can't change it; there are huge dynamics at play. Somebody said to me when I was frustrated a while back—I can't remember what story it was that I really wanted to see get more attention than it did—"Listen, while you were winning all those awards in the Syrian Civil War, when it was such a big story, there was probably some guy in Mexico getting shot at every other day, doing incredible work, and nobody was paying attention because Mexico wasn't a big story in that moment."

You do have to keep fighting for the stories you believe in, and trying to get them their inch of coverage, but also understand that you can't fight what people are interested in or drawn to at any given time.

EYE: Your book is *The Education of a Journalist*. But it's also the education of a reader; I didn't know a lot about the intricate details of what you write about.

CLARISSA: I want people to relate to this book on a human level because they're gripping stories. I'm so grateful to you for liking the book. There is no greater feeling than knowing that. You put yourself out there and when you feel that the story resonates with someone and the people and places, that for me is "the juice," as we say.

EYE: Thank you so much for giving your time to talk about all this, Clarissa. I have admired you from afar for many, many years.

First published in September, 2020.

Eleanor Clift

Eleanor Clift on Gabrielle Giffords and the Washington She Knows

By Pamela Burke

Eleanor Clift is a well-known Washington journalist whose insider reporting appears in *Newsweek* and the *Daily Beast*. You've probably seen her as a regular contributor to the nationally syndicated show *The McLaughlin Group*, firmly holding her own with the other vociferous panelists.

Her article "The Gabrielle Giffords I Know" in the *Daily Beast* caught my eye. The story that began as a memorial and ended as a tribute appeared the day the congresswoman was shot.

Eleanor recalled remarks Representative Gabby Giffords had made the week before on two panels they shared at Renaissance Weekend in South Carolina.

> "Gabby's attitude makes us appreciate our public servants. During the last election cycle or two, they've been the object of such animosity."
> —Eleanor Clift

I wanted to ask Eleanor about this personal story and get her reflections on Giffords and the country as the weeks have passed. She was kind enough to offer her observations...

EYE: We saw the empty seat left for Representative Giffords and the invited guests from Tucson at the State of the Union Speech. The photo of her and her husband holding hands at the Houston hospital was very touching. How did the shooting incident change business as usual in Washington?

ELEANOR: The shooting was a circuit breaker that prompted everybody to do some needed self-examination. The result is a renewed tone of civility. That doesn't mean the partisan fights are over, but there might be less name-calling.

EYE: I went to Tucson and was struck by the outpouring of support and love for Gabby.

ELEANOR: Yes, and this is a time when everyone is so critical of politicians. Everyone is rooting for her. She had a particularly warm and outgoing personality. It went across the ideological spectrum.

> That's her community and she really worked hard at her job there. Every weekend she did some kind of event.

We sometimes forget how close members of the House are to their constituents.

EYE: Why has this story touched such a nerve?

ELEANOR: Not only was it about Gabrielle Giffords, but there was the prospect that it was a political assassination attempt. And there was the fear that it was the direct result of political rhetoric. It's touched us on a number of levels.

The tragic death of the nine-year-old girl moved everyone. Gabrielle's heritage is Jewish. A Mexican-American intern saved her life. The trauma chief there is a Korean-American who served in Iraq and Afghanistan. The judge was a Roman Catholic who had been to Mass that morning. The story included a cross section of America that we should rightfully be proud of.

EYE: Your story about Giffords sharing her thoughts on the political climate was very illuminating. How did you happen to write about that conversation?

ELEANOR: I was sitting at home and had just filed a story for the *Daily Beast* on an upcoming lunch with the First Lady and Mrs. Carla Bruni-Sarcozy. Then I read in my email that there had been a shooting.

> **I saw that Gabby was involved and heard her pronounced dead. I was very upset. I had spent some time at three Renaissance Weekends with her and her husband Mark, and had gotten to know them.**

I told my editor that I had just seen her and that she talked about her most recent race. I also said that on a personal note, Gabby was one of the smartest, warmest, and most down-to-earth people I knew. He said to write the story as a memorial.

EYE: What happened when you found out she had survived the shooting?

ELEANOR: We immediately made it a tribute. I did say initially that these weekends are supposed to be off the record, but given what had happened, I felt it would be worthwhile to write about it.

What she said about the ugliness of the campaign was so poignant in the context of what had happened that I knew she would say it in a public forum. The amount of time members of Congress spend fundraising and the fact that her last race cost $4.2 million are not secrets either.

I have nothing but the highest praise for this woman. I also pointed out that she voted against Speaker Nancy Pelosi and for Congressman John Lewis. She is from a very difficult district. Nancy Pelosi did not hold that against her one bit.

EYE: Is Gabby an atypical politician in Washington?

ELEANOR: She really stands out amongst the 435 members in the House because she has such an exuberant personality. She has successfully navigated politics in a district where she's on the progressive side and the district is on the conservative side.

The two other women who flew out to see her also are standouts. Representative Debbie Wasserman Schultz from Florida was diagnosed with breast cancer and had a double mastectomy at 44. She spoke about it at a dinner last month and gave her thoughts on the GOP mantra for repealing Obamacare and replacing it with a plan of their own. Senator Kirsten Gillibrand from New York has also gravitated to Gabby.

EYE: Is there a new camaraderie amongst women in Congress in Washington?

ELEANOR: No. It's always been there. There are stories that go back before the Internet on how women, particularly in the Senate, came together. There was a women's caucus headed by former Representative Pat Schroeder from Colorado years ago. She and Senator Olympia Snowe co-chaired this pro-choice caucus.

EYE: There is something about Representative Giffords' dedication to the job that's been illuminating and invigorating.

ELEANOR: Gabby's attitude makes us appreciate our public servants. The last election cycle or two they've been the object of such animosity. If the new era of civility takes hold, people may look at them in a new way.

EYE: We were all taken by the photos of Gabby's husband holding her hand both in Houston and in Tucson. What do you think about their exposure to so much media?

ELEANOR: What they're going through is very private. In the months ahead, they will want their privacy more and more. I winced when I heard all the detail about her injuries, but this is the world we live in.

> **People want to know. I think they've done a good job so far balancing between the need to know and keeping what should be private, private.**

EYE: It seems like they have a wonderful relationship with an amazing closeness.

ELEANOR: They are close. One of the things she talked about at Renaissance was the terrible ads that were run that said, "Her husband won't even vote for her—why should we?" The reality was that his legal address was not in her district, so he *couldn't* vote for her.

He's stationed in Houston with two teenage daughters. She was quite concerned about the unfairness of the attack because it was completely false.

EYE: This is an unusual couple. They have a very different lifestyle and both have jobs in the spotlight.

ELEANOR: These are two very high-powered people from two very different walks of life who met on a visit to China. They reconnected when she was working on the issue of capital punishment at an Arizona state prison. That is an unusual courtship.

EYE: You started as a secretary at the beginning of your career. Did you always know you wanted to be a writer or reporter?

ELEANOR: The only time I was indispensable was when I was a secretary. I still can take shorthand and type up a storm. It never occurred to me that I could be a reporter.

I was working at *Newsweek* and saw that there was something else going on out there. That was the era when women were agitating. I never would have been the first one at the barricades.

EYE: You've come such a long way. Last year you lectured on Women in Politics at Stanford University. How did you finally become a journalist?

ELEANOR: The women at *Newsweek* brought a lawsuit against the company in the early '70s. As part of the settlement, *Newsweek* created internships for women to try out. I asked for one and got it. They assigned me to cover Jimmy Carter, who was running for president.

> **The tradition in journalism is that if you cover the winning candidate, you get to go to Washington. So that's how I got here, and I've been here ever since. I call that my Cinderella story.**

EYE: You're known for your honesty. How important is that in journalism?

ELEANOR: It makes better copy. It gives it authenticity. That's what people are looking for. It's a lot easier to be honest than to figure out tortured ways of covering up what the truth is. It works—and it's much better for your health.

EYE: You co-wrote a book called *Madam President, Shattering the Glass Ceiling* that examined the prospects for women seeking high office. Do you think there will be a female president soon?

ELEANOR: It's inevitable, but whether it's going to happen in the near or distant future is hard to tell. It's difficult to hone in on the specific woman it might be. Hillary Clinton could have another run in her. Someone like Senator Gillibrand is beginning to get a name for herself.

She certainly would have the time it takes to get there. It's very difficult to find a specific woman who would make it with all that it takes.

EYE: You make the point that a woman would govern differently. Can you expand on that?

ELEANOR: There have been all kinds of studies concluding that women are more collaborative and that they don't seem to care about who gets the credit. I think we can learn something by the way Hillary has been operating.

She handed off a lot of power at the State Department, yet she still has always managed to stay in control. I think women tend to be more collaborative as leaders. Janet Napolitano was very successful in Arizona. Look at Gabrielle Gifford's leadership style. She's very empathetic and reaches out. Men do that, too. But I think it tends to come more naturally to women.

EYE: Is there room for optimism now in Washington with the president [Obama] calling for civility and both sides of the aisle sitting together at the State of the Union Speech?

ELEANOR: Yes, because the Republicans now have some shared responsibility for governing. They can't just stay on the sidelines and throw spitballs.

EYE: You continue to write for *Newsweek* and the *Daily Beast* as they combine forces. Are you going to write another book?

ELEANOR: I probably will write a memoir telling my Cinderella story. Right now life is busy with blogging and the new news environment at *Newsweek* and the *Daily Beast*.

EYE: I was struck by the last line of your article: *What a terrible irony that her husband can go into space in a capsule and return home safely, but his wife's safety can't be assured outside a Safeway supermarket.* Can people feel safe anymore?

ELEANOR: I think people are more mindful that there can be violence and that there are deranged people out there. You wonder—if these were people we didn't know as well, and not a federal judge, a member of Congress, and a nine-year-old—whether the story would have gotten this kind of attention.

I think we have these kinds of things happen periodically. We're not going to put up metal detectors everywhere.

EYE: Thanks, Eleanor, for your terrific insight. We're looking forward to reading your next articles and particularly that future memoir.

First Published in January, 2011.

Kim Covington

Broadcaster-Turned-Activist Kim Covington: From Finding Golden Nuggets to Serving the Community

By *Catherine Anaya*

Kim Covington is a woman who wears many hats. She's a former television reporter, an anchor at several stations across America during her 30-year broadcast career and always had a passion for journalism.

> "Everyone has a story. I love telling stories. I love people and what I love more than anything is finding solutions to a problem."
>
> —*Kim Covington*

Kim was seriously injured in a traffic accident a few years ago while she was covering the news. In time she recovered from the horrible incident, and in the process decided to answer what she describes as a new calling: to concentrate her time and attention on community advocacy.

She created her own company, the Covington Companies, where she focuses on her passion for education and philanthropy.

We talked about life after television, her roles as a mom and wife, and her new direction...

EYE: First, I want to talk about your career, because you left TV after 30 years. It was actually in 2015, the same time I did. What was it about TV news that drew you into it to begin with?

KIM: I love finding solutions. I covered a segment here in Phoenix called School Solutions. I wasn't so much looking for the problems in education but what worked.

> **And I loved that. I'd loved searching for the truth, finding the golden nugget and telling people's stories. And also, I'm just nosy, you know.**

I like to get the information before anyone else and then share it and say *Look at what I found!* I love to write. I'm a storyteller; I *love* telling stories! My whole life, that's what I've enjoyed.

I started in radio. Did you know that in high school we had a little radio station? I was drawn to that. In ninth grade, my teacher said I should go to journalism school. I was like, *What is that?* So I was introduced to journalism school then.

EYE: Now, did you have this perfect voice back then?

KIM: They said I did. I just loved to talk. My dad has this really deep voice. He sings in a choir. We were always singing in the gospel choir so I was always told I had a great singing voice. But I never really realized that until I started working.

EYE: You knew early on what you wanted to do. You worked in TV markets like Grand Rapids, Michigan, and Springfield and St. Louis, Missouri, where you're from. You've said that community advocacy was always important to you.

KIM: I always had one foot embedded in the community working with nonprofits and one foot in news. I could never just put a story to bed. I always wondered what happened after, you know, *How can we save these children? What can we do? What's available to help this family?*

> That's always been a part of my work. I never really separated it. So I was always burning candles at both ends. That's why it was an easy transition from television news to community service and philanthropy.

It was easy for me to get a job at the Arizona Community Foundation because that's really the work

I've been doing my entire career, whether it was in Springfield, Grand Rapids, St. Louis or in Phoenix.

EYE: Let's talk about why you decided to leave. You were involved in a serious traffic accident while you were covering news. What happened? How bad were your injuries?

KIM: I don't remember the actual accident. We were on our way to an education story, and we were downtown riding in a news vehicle. A woman was on her cell phone—not paying attention—and slammed into my side of the vehicle. Thank God I was in a safety belt.

> **My photographer said he saw it happen. She slammed into the news vehicle. We rolled into oncoming traffic. It hit my side of the car again. Everyone walked away from the accident but me. The photographer thought I was dead.**

EYE: How horrible! What happened after that?

KIM: My eyes were open; blood was rushing from my head. So he believed I had died. He called it in and said, "She's dead. What do I do?" He panicked. The assignment desk called 9-1-1.

The police officers arrived. The sergeant at the time said the officers called it in as a possible fatality, but bring the jaws of life anyway. He told me never to listen to that 9-1-1 tape. And I've always been afraid to.

And so they pulled me out. Almost half the newsroom came to the scene, including the news director who was in the ambulance. And that's when I awakened. I don't remember, but they said I apologized for all the mess I had made.

That's the funny part. When we got to the emergency room, all I could remember was my husband's face. And I said, "All this must be more than a scratch." A police officer who had heard about the accident on the scanner said he felt compelled to come to the emergency room and pray with me.

So he prayed a prayer. All I remember was "In Jesus' name, Amen."

EYE: Did you know him before?

KIM: I did not know him. We were reunited six months later and we just wept on the phone. I get tears just remembering. There were so many people who prayed for me. It was literally the darkest hour of my life.

EYE: People who were around at that time in the midst of it say it's amazing you're still alive. You suffered a traumatic concussion. Your recovery was a long process.

KIM: Yes, a traumatic brain injury. Thank God the hospital was so close. And thank God for the surgeon, Dr. Steven Erickson.

Right after the surgery, they came to my bedside and said, "She is suffering from traumatic brain injury; we must treat her immediately." They saved my eyes. I could not focus. I would black out every time I moved my head.

My speech had changed. I could not read. It's very difficult to explain what happens to the brain when it gets shaken up. And mine had gotten shaken up at least three times. When a football player gets hit, well, he has a helmet on. I did not. And so it took nine months to get my head on straight.

And there were other injuries. I couldn't move my arms. I had deep injuries, deep cuts to the muscles and my hands and my ear and all that. They had to put my ear back on, for example. It was a lot more serious than we ever described.

EYE: This is the first time I am learning just how serious it was.

KIM: I tried to go back after nine months. I started working in the newsroom part time, and I did that for about a year. I tried.

EYE: Did you feel like you couldn't do the job, or your heart just wasn't there anymore?

KIM: Both. I could not physically get into a news vehicle anymore without being totally traumatized. So I was driving myself to live shots. And then I lost the passion. And when you lose the passion for that industry—which is already hard—you don't need that, too, you know?

> **I still enjoy that medium because it is so powerful. I miss that. But the passion wasn't there. I knew that once I walked into the newsroom, I knew it was not my calling anymore. I had a different calling after that.**

EYE: So tell me about this new calling, because I read where you've described it saying you just knew this was what you wanted to do. You had to be in the community and advocate for it and help philanthropies. You started your company. But how did you know that was it for you?

KIM: As I mentioned before, my heart was always in two different places, in the news or in the community.

But I was afraid, you know. You get sucked into television and that paycheck. That keeps you there a little bit longer. And before you know it, it's been 30 years.

EYE: But there's something odd about suffering through trauma; it makes you appreciate that life is too short and you have to let go of the fear.

KIM: And there's such a great need there. I learned so much in news about poverty. I could not look away. I knew there was a place where I could be of greater service and that was the Arizona Community Foundation. They know how to do it right. It is the state's largest grantmaker, the largest private provider of scholarships.

> We cover all of Arizona. There is probably not one nonprofit that hasn't been served by the Community Foundation. There are so many generous people in Arizona. They will drop everything to support people. It is a beautiful experience. It is so purposeful.

We match donors to the need. I go out as Senior Director of Community Initiatives and assess the need. I see where we need it and we help either find a grant or convene and show other people what's going on so we can collaboratively, collectively, support that need.

We know that there is a big refugee crisis right now. They need more support. There are huge education gaps. We know that we're always going to need help to fill the gaps in education, health and HIV prevention. We know that among African-Americans and Latinos, it is off the charts. So if you know, you've got to do something!

EYE: I love the work you're doing. We talk a lot about education. You know Arizona ranks toward the bottom of the list of states when it comes to educational success. I know education has been a focus of yours for a very long time. What are we missing? What do we need?

KIM: We need to support our teachers. Why would they do missionary work? Many teachers are working two jobs. They are bunking in with other teachers because they can't make the rent. And yet we're asking them to prepare our children for college and careers. We don't treat teachers as if they are in an honored profession, but they are.

EYE: I want to touch on an issue because I know that we women in news have always had a hard time chasing the elusive balance between career and motherhood. Do you feel like you finally found it?

KIM: You know, I found it and then I lost it again. You get so wrapped up in the community and there are so many people pulling at you. I have an 11-year old, a 12-year-old and a husband. They say, "Remember TV? Don't do it again. You know, you had a hard time finding that balance and we don't want to be put on a things-to-do list." And I don't want them to be there.

> So it's constant, constant. You have to be very, very in tune with what's going on every single day. You can't take a break from what you need to get done each day—and that is putting your family first.

EYE: I applaud you for that, Kim. Thank you so much for being with me on The Women's Eye!

First published in April, 2017.

Lee Woodruff

Lee Woodruff on Family, Creating a Foundation and Her Reinvention

By Stacey Gualandi

Lee Woodruff knows what it means to overcome adversity. Five years ago her husband, ABC anchor Bob Woodruff, suffered a near-fatal brain injury from a roadside bomb while reporting from Iraq. It has been a long, yet successful, road to recovery. In the process, she has become a voice for brain-injured soldiers returning from war.

> "Things happen in life and we need to reach out and seek help."
>
> —Lee Woodruff

Lee and her husband wrote *In An Instant*, an instant bestseller about healing from such a horrible event. They formed the Bob Woodruff Foundation to help raise awareness, money, and assistance to troops in recovery.

In her follow-up book, *Perfectly Imperfect, A Life in Progress,* Lee humorously tackled the subject of everyday challenges. She also speaks tirelessly to people all over the country. This *Good Morning America* correspondent will soon be one of the hosts at the More Magazine Reinvention Convention in Los Angeles.

I have recently had to "reinvent" myself, so I was very interested in talking with Lee about how to move forward and find inner strength...

EYE: You have a real knack for turning adversity into advantage...would you agree?

LEE: I guess so. A 75-year-old cancer survivor said to me you have two choices when something bad happens: You can get bitter or get better.

> **So when you take something bad that's happened and do something good with it and it impacts even one person, you're doing something to help yourself heal.**

EYE: Have your writing and speaking appearances helped you to adapt and ultimately help others in the process?

LEE: Yes. I tell my story, but I always try to put attention back to our wounded warriors who have returned home, and their families. They've not only paid the ultimate sacrifice by losing a family member but have suffered the sometimes equally painful sacrifice of a traumatic brain injury (TBI).

That's when a husband or spouse can be in a wheelchair and nonverbal, suffering from post-traumatic stress disorder or PTSD. One of the hidden aspects of injuries is that someone may look OK on the outside, but inside the basic wounds of war are really hard to heal without appropriate treatment.

EYE: You and Bob started the Bob Woodruff Foundation. Do you think you've raised awareness about our soldiers and head injuries?

LEE: I'd like to think so. I think America needs to be wakened up more and remember that these families are out there. Our Executive Director says, "Some of us went to war, some of us went shopping." Less than 1% are serving in a volunteer army.

> **It's really easy to forget there are people out there every day. Bob and I always say that this isn't a political issue. It's really about how a country takes care of its own when they've been asked to go, and they've stood up.**

EYE: Is this a situation where if people aren't directly affected by it, they sort of deny it?

LEE: That's such a good point. I recently heard someone say that if we keep up all this strife and the crises in Libya, etc., we're out of troops! We're sending them back six and seven times. If there were a senator's son drafted, maybe we'd be more thoughtful about the areas of conflict we're getting involved in.

EYE: How are you and Bob and your family doing five years later?

LEE: I think we're doing well. I don't ask a lot of questions of my kids. Someday I think I'll ask at Thanksgiving dinner, "Ok, kids, how was that whole experience for you? Ha! How badly are you going to need a therapist?" At the time I was telling myself *You're doing the best you can.*

I had tremendous amounts of help and support from everywhere. People are amazing in a crisis in so many ways. The kids are good. And Bob is back on television.

EYE: So many people have watched him and can't believe he went through such a traumatic brain injury and survived.

LEE: I love hearing people say to me, "I saw him on TV and that's the guy hit by a bomb?"

EYE: Explain exactly what the Bob Woodruff Foundation does. You talk about the experience of being a caregiver.

LEE: We looked at all our own experiences at Bethesda Naval Hospital and saw the care given to these individuals was really exceptional, every step of the way. But once they are discharged and on to the next phase of rehabilitation through the VA system, that may not be convenient for everyone.

There are a lot of struggles. The government and the VA have picked their game up in the last five years. Nobody was prepared for this; in other wars, they didn't survive TBIs like Bob's.

That became the impetus for us to create a foundation that would look at everyone out there on the ground, those small grassroots organizations doing good work.

We would raise money and awareness, and make grants to organizations to assist and act as a United Way, if you will, for military causes—like camp to help children heal because they wonder *Why is daddy different?*

EYE: When a soldier is injured, that injury affects everyone they know…

LEE: Yes. Bob's brother said, "It's not just Bob who got hit by a bomb, it's all of us." The ripple effect touches everyone in the family.

EYE: You have this infectious energy and sense of fun. Have you had low moments? You never seem like you get down or depressed.

LEE: That's so nice! I write about that in *Perfectly Imperfect*. I describe the recovery process where everyone leaves the driveway, and then you crash as a caretaker. I totally crashed. I wrote honestly about situational depression, having to be patient to help this man heal.

It's worse than watching paint dry. I talk about antidepressants and going to talk to someone. I want to let people know that when big things happen, it's not their fault.

> **Things happen in life and we need to reach out and seek help. It is possible, and there should be no stigma.**

EYE: Do you think you're a role model in that respect? People see and hear you and think, *If she can do it, so can I.*

LEE: If I do nothing else—and I'm probably the most imperfect person out there—if I can show people I'm a mom and I had this big thing happen …

EYE: You're real!

LEE: That is probably the highest compliment you can pay someone. If that helps people understand that they can do it, then I'm in!

EYE: You are one of the hosts for the More Reinvention Convention. What will that be like?

LEE: It is for people at that point in life when they are deciding they want to reinvent themselves, maybe go back to work, change their work. There will be amazing speakers, and I'll be the glue holding it together: Rita Wilson, Malaak Compton-Rock, they're the superstars who will share.

EYE: How do you like the title of role model?

LEE: I'm a messy person. I can say we are all built to survive. We are resilient. If you're in your dark moments, I promise you will laugh again. And you will touch joy again in your heart. These things are possible! If I can be a role model in that way then I'm honored.

EYE: You make reinvention interesting. Bob's injury changed your life. What does the concept of reinvention mean?

LEE: I hope we constantly reinvent ourselves as we get older, wiser and find new passions. I would hope that life is a constant set of reinventions. I'm an example of how bad things can thrust you into an ability to reinvent. I spent years running a PR/marketing firm, and wrote when I could.

I always wanted to write a book when kids were gone because it does require focus. *In An Instant* was written as a journal to process what was going on. *Perfectly Imperfect* has stories that connect women. And now I just wrote my first novel. I always envisioned that as a little girl.

> **By stepping out of my comfort zone, I ended up speaking in front of people. As a PR person, I was fine writing the story about someone else, and that's what is so ironic now. That's reinvention—tapping into where you are at that point in your life.**

EYE: How hard is it to reinvent? Is it for everyone?

LEE: Not everyone talks about taking calculated risks. At the More Convention, you can get useful information to use if you're serious about reinvention.

EYE: You're really busy! Mother of four, writer, you speak 100 times a year and you have the Stand Up For Heroes Event to benefit the Bob Woodruff Foundation coming up. Are you wearing too many hats?

LEE: I woke up at age 50 and realized that I must like

my life that way, and I work best when I have lists of things to accomplish and am operating on a high level of adrenaline.

EYE: You talk so highly of Bob. What would Bob say about you?

LEE: He is very complimentary of me. His television producers always ask me when he's in a bar in a foreign country, "Where can we find someone like Bob because women are always trying to pick him up and all he talks about is how much he loves you?!"

So I'll let it go when his underwear is on the floor two feet from the laundry basket! Haha!!

EYE: When we talk about our passions, what are you most passionate about: writing, speaking…?

LEE: My perfect dream world would be to wake up to no emails in my inbox, and just write for three hours straight without having to talk to people. Then go out after and have lots of interaction. That would be perfect.

EYE: Lee, you are my hero!! I look forward to talking with you again when your first novel comes out next spring, if not sooner. Continued success to you and Bob!

First published in May, 2011.

Part V
Impacters:
Inspiring Their Readers

"Storytelling is the most powerful way to
put ideas into the world today."

—*Robert McAfee Brown*, Educator and Author

Laura Munson

Writing Retreat Leader Laura Munson on Starting a New Movement for Women at their "Now What?" Crossroads

By Stacey Gualandi

New York Times bestselling author Laura Munson and I first met about nine years ago during the massive international success of her very first memoir, *This Is Not The Story You Think It Is*. We talked about being an author, starring as the main character in her own book and teaching Haven Writing Retreats at her Whitefish, Montana, home.

> "This time I am not the main character in the book...I know that book helped a lot of people, but this one is going to help a lot of people too. It's a delight to be able to shine its light on the important message of women supporting women, coming together in community."
>
> —*Laura Munson*

Laura is with me again to talk this time about her brand-new book called *Willa's Grove*, a novel she hopes will start a new women's movement and will encourage women to tell their own stories...

EYE: The whole backdrop of your new book is Montana, and Montana is definitely your muse, right?

LAURA: Yes. I never ever dreamed that I'd end up living here, but it's been almost 30 years. I've raised two kids here and this is where I call home. It offers up a massive dose of inspiration to my muse every day.

EYE: Since you were 18 you've been writing novels. So this is something that I think is really special for you.

LAURA: I've been writing novels since I got out of college, and realized that I was not in fact an actress but a writer.

> **That meant I had to really stand at the intersection of heart and craft and mind that is the writing life for many years before it was time to start sending books out.**

I have about five to eight novels that I think are ready to go, but I really wanted the book that followed my memoir to be more current. So I worked on this novel for about seven to eight years, and I'm really proud of it. It's inspired by what I see happen at Haven Writing Retreats.

EYE: I feel like on some level you are pulling from your own life.

LAURA: You know, writers, whether they write fiction or nonfiction, are always mining our lives. I like to say to people that the women in this book are nobody I know, none of them is me, and yet they're all of us.

> **Every issue these women are dealing with is an issue that somebody you love or know, if not yourself, has dealt with or will deal with.**

EYE: The sense of community seems important to you.

LAURA: The book started as a call to action, to show people the power of what can happen when we leave our daily lives in order to create a new kind of community, a temporary community, a *bridge community* I call it, in order to help each other move forward in life.

Haven is a writing retreat, using the power of self-expression to help people move forward in their lives. But this book in no way is a retreat. It is about four women taking a break from their lives who all are at major crossroads moments, and they need to answer the burning question we all ask, and that's, *"So now, what?"*

EYE: These four women get together and they're all dealing with a lot of trauma, but they break it down. Then they're at this low point, and then I feel like through the power of the friendship, they build themselves all back up again to say, *Okay, we're ready to move on from this.* Is that right?

LAURA: Absolutely! The way they help each other, the way they create this bond, is by telling each other their stories. I think so many of us, when going through crossroads moments with big decisions to make, we tend to isolate. We tend to become islands because we feel the people in our daily lives might judge us.

This book models women who are all in isolation, who realize that they need to come together and tell each other their stories.

So the way it works is that Willa, who's in fact the protagonist, finally comes clean and calls a childhood friend and says, "I can't do this alone anymore. I've got to figure out the next chapter of my life."

That character says, "Almost every woman I know is in the same sort of crossroads." It might just be a different issue, but you know, they've got these decisions to make. Why don't you invite me? Then I'll invite somebody who's also at a major crossroads, and she invites a fourth, and then we'll all come together.

So while the book takes place in Montana, and Montana really is a character in the book, these are women from four really different demographics.

EYE: You're obviously telling a story and you want it to get it right, but is there a reason why it took seven years to get this finally finished?

LAURA: That's a great question. When I wrote the memoir, I was writing my way through a marital crisis. Life gave me a six-month marital crisis, so it was the perfect container for a memoir. Finding the container for a novel, crafting a novel, creating characters that have beating hearts even though you've imagined them, takes some time. So the book that is currently in print is probably the 19th draft.

EYE: It's constantly evolving for you, too.

LAURA: It's my true love. I've been writing books, book after book, for years. Some of them are even good. I say that writing is my practice, my prayer, my meditation, my way of life, and sometimes my way to life.

With over a thousand alums from all over the world, I've seen my writer's retreat change people's lives over and over again. I had to ask myself, *Do I have a community like this where I'm not the leader?* I think in many ways, and this was done very subconsciously, this was my way of creating a community that felt safe to me.

EYE: Did you set out to have this theme of women helping women, because you say sometimes we all become islands?

LAURA: Yes. I'm totally dedicated to this. What I'm hoping is that people will read the book, and then say, "You know what I want to do? I want to host a week-long retreat like this, up at my lake house in Wisconsin, and call it Stacey's Grove. The book begins with an invitation that starts, "You are invited to the rest of your life."

> I think it's time that we say, "Yes," to the profound invitations of our lives. That's what these characters do. Now, some of them resist it.

This sort of stuff doesn't come naturally to us. In fact, there's a line in the book that says something like, you know we're all fluent in this language, the language of community. It really is our mother tongue, yet we so rarely speak it.

EYE: Does getting away help people have these types of conversations?

LAURA: This book is about the conversations that are possible when people get that real, and that raw, and when they're that deliberate with the expressed intention of moving forward in their lives—something happens.

But it doesn't happen when we isolate at home, and hide and pretend. So I'm making a case for reaching out, coming together. There's a great line that the poet Emma Melon uses in one of her poems, and it says, "Allow yourself to be spelled differently." I think coming to a place like Montana, where most people haven't been before, can really inspire that kind of transformation.

EYE: This is a very different kind of week, isn't it?

LAURA: I call it a bridge community. I'm not making a case for leaving home and not relying on your family and your friends. That's not it at all. But I am making a case for sometimes going someplace very far outside of our comfort zone, and getting real.

> That's what happens for these women. It's like they're bridging. As they become islands, they now bridge to one another in a new place, in a new community, so that they can bridge to themselves, and more powerfully bridge back to their daily lives.

EYE: Willa, the main character, says she's a firm believer in storytelling. Are you yourself a firm believer in storytelling? Why do you think it's so important now in this day and age?

LAURA: I remember in high school I used to say, *If you can't be vulnerable, I don't want to be your friend.* That, of course, sent people running in the opposite direction. But I've always prized vulnerability, and honesty, and storytelling.

Brené Brown has turned this into something that's really alive and well in our collective right now, and so important. There were times when I was writing where I thought, *Man, there's a lot of talking in the first hundred pages; that's what they're there to do.*

I started to resist it. Then I realized, it's the people who think there's a lot of talking in this book at the beginning, who are the exact people who need to be having those conversations.

> But so often we just tidy up our issues, and say, *Oh, on to the next, everything's fine.* We're bleeding inside. These women, they bleed together in their storytelling and in their sharing, which is so critical.

EYE: You talked about vulnerability. How are you feeling now because you had success with the memoir?

Do you judge your next book on it, or is this one a whole different thing? You're putting it out there, and now people are going to read it and you can't do anything about it.

LAURA: It's like if you have a biological child, and you give birth to that child, and you're alone with that child in a hospital room, or in your home if it's a home birth, and it's just you and that baby. That's what it's like when you're creating a book.

Then it comes time to pass the baby around, and then everybody wants to count its fingers and toes, and report on whether it looks like your Great-Aunt Eleanor or not. Then it's no longer all yours, and it becomes its own entity.

EYE: With the memoir, you said you needed to provide relief to yourself and to other people. What do you think is the mission for you with this novel?

LAURA: I finally realized that what my memoir is about is the possibility of emotional liberation. That we don't have to be victims emotionally of the things people say and do to us. How do we do that? Well, by becoming aware of our minds, and how our thought patterns both serve us and sabotage us.

That awareness changed my life. It changed that time in my life depicted in the book, and it changed my life in the years following it, and still does.

EYE: So telling stories can bring people self-awareness?

LAURA: This constant tuning in to how the mind works is still similar in theme to what happens in *Willa's Grove* because they are telling each other their stories, and speaking their stories brings them into a new level of self-awareness and truth.

Everything I do is about that. Every writing prompt I offer on my retreats, every conversation I have, one-on-ones, coaching, editing, all of it, is about helping people raise their self-awareness.

> **This time in this book, it's about how safe community, intentional community, can do just that.**

My next book will be about self-expression. It's as much about writing as it is about the way we express ourselves in general, and how to find that authentic, unique, surprising and essential way that only you can express yourself.

EYE: Wishing you great luck on that one. Wonderful to catch up with you again, Laura. Congratulations on all that you do to help people go on to success from your writing retreats. We look forward to your future books!

First published in March, 2020.

Laurie Burrows Grad and Peter Grad

Blogger Laurie Burrows Grad on Grief, Widowhood and Recovering from Tragic Loss

By Stacey Gualandi

Laurie Grad is changing the way we address an oftentimes taboo topic—surviving grief. She's well-known as a food writer and cookbook author. But when Peter, her beloved husband of 47 years, died suddenly in 2015, Laurie channeled her loss into a popular *Huffington Post*-like grief blog.

> "Writing was the thing that saved me. The pain made it come out of me and then onto the computer. Being able to get it onto the internet was even better."
> —*Laurie Burrows Grad*

She turned her blog into a book called *The Joke's Over, You Can Come Back Now*. The blog continues to help readers survive their own personal struggles. How Laurie plowed through her own grief and survived is a heartbreaking love story, but she does, somehow, with her sense of humor intact…

EYE: I have to thank you for doing this. Like I said, no matter how painful this whole experience has been for you, you really have kept that sense of humor.

LAURIE: I come from comedy. My father, Abe Burrows, was a comedy genius and my brother James, who is a television director and co-created *Cheers,* is also, so I guess it's in my blood.

EYE: That certainly has helped you get through this. How do you describe your husband Peter?

LAURIE: My best friend, my lover. We used to say people would ask us how our marriage stayed so long. And do you remember in *City Slickers* how Billy Crystal would hold up the one finger? The thing was to be able to say to someone, I might be wrong.

> And that's what kept us going. Because we would listen to each other and we would understand the love and not jump on each other. And that was sacred to our marriage. And that's what stayed with us for 47 years.

EYE: Was it almost like you were bonded for life?

LAURIE: And we were. He was my best friend. I called him five times a day. He called me five times a day. It was a big adjustment. I not only lost my husband, but I lost my status. My first blog was called

Demoted to Lunch. I realized that a widow was demoted to lunch.

> And I said, no, I have to teach the world.
> This can't be. It doesn't have to be that way.

EYE: You write in your book and your blog that you were unexpectedly thrust into widowhood. What do you mean by that?

LAURIE: Peter had been sick on and off all his life, but he always bounced back. We never thought he would die. You just don't think about it. Nobody thinks about it. And then he dropped dead in front of me.

We were on vacation in Vail, Colorado, and we were staying at somebody's house. In the middle of the night, he woke up and said, "I can't breathe. I can't breathe." And I said, "Stay with me." And I called 9-1-1. The people tried to get help there. And I said, "What's my name?" And he said, "Laurie," and I said, "What's my name?"

So he died in front of me. I knew he was one of those people who said the minute I go, put me down. He was gone in seconds. He must have had a massive heart attack.

EYE: You can't prepare for something like this. It's like the life that you knew has completely changed.

You write about this, but it's like you have no control anymore.

LAURIE: You don't. You don't eat. You're cooking for one all of a sudden. You're not interested in food. You can't sleep. So much of your life is upended. You're a single person. And couples don't ask you out because you're a fifth wheel.

You can't pick up a check. It's so bizarre. And you need to marshal your resources and figure out what to do. Somebody came to me and said *You should go see a medium.* I would see an extra small before I would see a medium. There was no way I was seeing a medium.

But everybody had advice. They would tell me *He's in a better place.* And I would say to them *Forget it, the better place would be playing golf or right beside me.* Or they would say that everything happens for a reason. Claptrap.

EYE: Does crying help to ease the pain?

LAURIE: *You'll get through it,* they said. *Be strong.* You can't be strong. You have to cry. And we have discovered through much research that tears have an emotional component in them that helps you survive this. It's good to cry; it's important to cry. The more tears, the better.

One of the worst things that someone can say is *I know how you feel*. I would not have written if it hadn't been for Sheryl Sandberg's treatise 30 days after her husband had died. I knew she could write, so I decided to write.

You say *I'm sorry for your loss* or you just sit with someone. You don't ask them what you can do for them because deciding anything is impossible. So you just say, *I'm bringing you dinner*. Or just say nothing and give the person a hug because they get no hugs.

EYE: It's interesting when you mention people saying I'm so sorry for your loss. My dad died in 2009, not unexpectedly as my dad had cancer (my parents were married for 47 years), but it still was very tough. The one thing that my mother did not like people saying to her was *I'm so sorry for your loss*. She said, *If I hear that one more time...* She just got sick of it.

LAURIE: You know, Stacey, I've discovered from talking to other widows, all death is sudden. The other thing I've learned is you don't lose someone like you lose your keys; you expect to find them.

There is an expectation. And if you say *I lost my husband*, it's as if you did something wrong that you let him go. It makes you feel bad that you lost your husband.

So you've experienced a loss, but you didn't lose him. He passed a football, he passed the gravy. But he did not pass. He died. I've got to insist that people use the "D" word.

EYE: You are also saying not to sugarcoat it. See it as it is.

LAURIE: And doctors don't know how to do that. I have been lecturing to doctors through this grief center I'm a part of, teaching them to use the "D" word.

EYE: It's almost like you have to just face it head-on, no matter how difficult that is. Your book started as a series of blogs that you wrote. You said that creating meaning from loss was your resurrection from the debris of your heartache.

LAURIE: I think that journaling is a big help to widows because they can see their progress. You can't write on day one, but you can start writing maybe on day 14, and then you can look back in three months and say, *Oh, my gosh, I am doing better.* That's where writing is really helpful.

EYE: What's the feedback that you've gotten?

LAURIE: The first blog went viral on the Huffington Post and Arianna Huffington was very kind. She tweeted it. And I think we had 10,000 hits the first day on Facebook. Yes, there was a need for it.

EYE: Now you've not only been thrust into widowhood but you're into being an expert on the subject to try to change the fact that grief is such a forbidden topic. What's it going to take for us to use the "D" word?

LAURIE: I'm trying. It's really hard. However, what I found comforting was cooking; it had been my expertise. I couldn't cook at first at all. And then people would take me out to dinner. And then I decided that I had to pay them back.

And I started to cook. For me, it was very comforting. Then all of a sudden the freezer would get full of things. And for me, cooking was love and I could at least feed myself and feed others.

> It takes a while until you can feed yourself with self-compassion and you can feed others. That is a way towards recovery. We use the word *restoration*.

EYE: Many people know you also as this awesome cookbook author. You've included recipes to help one deal with grief.

LAURIE: I have nine recipes in the book and my famous brownies. They are comforting. I even got a tattoo. It's a heart. It says LBG loves PG, as if you'd carved it in a tree. It's on my wrist. I touch it all the time. Everybody thought I was off my rocker. I loved it.

EYE: Is this your path? What do you call it? The new normal?

LAURIE: I call it acceptably different. Normal died with Peter. It's a big adjustment. Normal is a relative term. What was normal is no longer normal. What was normal was our future. And we no longer have a future. So I had to find my own future.

EYE: Many people don't date after their new normal. Dating is something you address in the book.

LAURIE: Yes, I went to lunch on this date and I was looking fine. And I said, "I hear you're 70." He said, "No, I lied." I said, "I hear you're a liberal." He said, "No, I'm a staunch Republican." I said, "I hear you like to cook." He said, "No, I hate it." And I walked out of the restaurant.

So I decided not to use the web or any of these services. It's been almost three years now. Even though I have a major in melancholy and a minor in sadness, how many times can I rely on Amazon Echo and Siri for my company?

EYE: You said, too, that you'll never lose your connection and continuing bond with Peter.

LAURIE: You definitely have a continuing bond. Freud in 1917 said that we should sever all bonds. He felt that once you sever the bond, you could find a new relationship. But what they've discovered (and I think was in a book called *Continuing Bonds*) is that you have to keep the bonds. And I find that most widows enjoy keeping the bond. I talk to Peter all the time.

EYE: Tell us about your best advice to people who might be going through this, especially when it's still extremely raw.

LAURIE: I think to find self-compassion. It's a really hard thing to go deep and find self-compassion because you're hurting so much, and you've got guilt about how your spouse died.

> **I think the first thing to do is to find a grief center. I not only found Our House, a grief support center in Los Angeles, but I went through a group there.**

I am now on their board. I'm going to give a percentage of my proceeds from the book to them because they were so helpful.

I think finding support, be it private or group-related, is really key. You figure out very early on who's going to stand by you. Peter used to call me five times a day. One of my friends, Diane, ends up calling me five times a day. She knew I needed it, became my sister and has been fabulous.

My son has been wonderful and my grandkids are fabulous. And I think also reading books, reading memoirs of other people going through it is amazingly cathartic because you know you're not alone. When I went into group, I was saying, *Why me!* And then you go, *Why not me?*

> **So you have the feeling that you're among others. If you can't do a group, read the books. A lot of widows have said that they keep my book on their nightstand.**

EYE: Are you sick and tired of being a widow? Are you going to keep writing, keeping an update?

LAURIE: I'm going to keep writing, but I am sick and tired of being a widow.

EYE: I want to thank you so much for your warmth, your wisdom and your wit. Please keep making us laugh, Laurie. But again, the book is *The Joke's Over*.

First published in May, 2018.

In Memory of
Cokie Roberts
(1943-2019)

Cokie Roberts

Cokie Roberts Celebrates the Triumphs of Our Courageous Founding Mothers

By Stacey Gualandi

We have pioneer journalist Cokie Roberts to thank for giving us a new understanding of the intrepid and fearless women of the American Revolution. This accomplished *ABC News* and *NPR* political commentator is now a children's book author and has penned *Founding Mothers, Remembering the Ladies*.

> "I think the women of the Revolutionary Period would be flabbergasted that we have not come farther...It would equally amaze them that we have not had a woman president."
>
> —*Cokie Roberts*

Cited one of the 50 greatest women in the history of broadcasting by the American Women in Radio and Television, Cokie spent more than 40 years in the industry. She has many bestselling books under her belt, but with her new book, we and the kids discover the extraordinary triumphs of the women of the Revolution...

EYE: When I read this book, it was so refreshing to get a history lesson. It takes me right back to sixth grade when I played Martha Washington in the play *1776*. But I didn't know any of this history about Martha!

COKIE: Well, at least it was something. *1776* is a delightful play and it gives you some sense of Abigail Adams' letters as well. Most kids don't get that far, so you were ahead of the game.

EYE: I'm no kid, but I loved this book because there was so much history we didn't learn. You wrote an adult book about the same thing. Is that lack of information why you wrote it?

COKIE: Absolutely. The "grown up book," as I've come to call it, was also for that the reason. I didn't know about these women. And if I, who care so much about women and politics, didn't know anything about them, I figured other people would be even more ignorant.

> **That turned out to be the case. I set out about the incredibly hard work of learning about them. It's detective work. People have not kept or properly preserved the papers, letters or artifacts of these women.**

EYE: You profile Abigail Adams, Martha Washington, Dolley Madison, and others like Eliza Pinckley whom I had never heard of. How long did it take you to delve deeply into these women's lives?

COKIE: *Founding Mothers* came out in 2004 and then the sequel, *Ladies of Liberty,* in 2008. So, I'd say, between the two of them, it was about 10 years. The children's book was nowhere near as arduous in terms of time because I'd already done the research.

The person who spent incredible amounts of time on the children's book is the fabulous illustrator, Diane Goode, who has done an unbelievable job. She's a Caldecott Medal winner and really gets into her subject wonderfully. The drawings are whimsical and funny.

EYE: You had never written a children's book before. Was it difficult to adapt to a younger audience?

COKIE: I spend a lot of time with kids. I have six grandkids who are in this age group. I have a very good children's book editor at Harper Books, so that helped a lot.

> The truth is that being a broadcast journalist was the best preparation because I am used to having to make things very succinct and boil a whole of information down to very few words.

EYE: Whom were you most shocked to learn about in terms of their story?

COKIE: I don't think there was anybody I was most shocked about. What I found surprising was how deeply, deeply political these women were. First of all, our impressions are so different from that. They were sitting at home tending to their duties. Secondly, it was so difficult for them to be this political.

> **Just getting through the day in the 18th century was no piece of cake. These women were raising children, taking care of old people and all of that. A disease could come through and take two of your children in a week.**

With all of that, they, first of all, found the time and then the interest to be so deeply committed to the American cause. Abigail Adams said, "We women are really better patriots than you men." She said, "Here we are making all the sacrifices and suffering all the hardships for the cause, and if we win, you men are going to be held in high acclaim and hold office and we won't even be able to vote. So we are better patriots than you are."

EYE: Didn't John Adams kind of laugh at his wife?

COKIE: No. On that letter he agreed with her. She then told him to remember the ladies when they formed a new code of laws, and he did in fact laugh at her.

EYE: And thus the title of your book. I was most amazed by Deborah Franklin, who was married to Benjamin Franklin. For the majority of the marriage, he was in Europe, making her, actually, the Post Master General!

COKIE: Yes, that's right! She really was. That's one of the first things you learn in school, that Benjamin Franklin was the first Post Master General of the United States. But, he wasn't here. He was in England. And, by the way, he was having a very nice time there. And she was running the Postal Service and their businesses.

They had, essentially, a Kinkos. He thought she did a wonderful job. He would say, "Oh, you're really good at this, Deborah." That was fine; she could do all that, but she wanted him home. He was gone for years at a time.

Their only daughter got married and he still wouldn't come because he wanted to keep the wedding cheap. He was a lobbyist for Pennsylvania and for the colonies in England. At one point his neighbors thought he had been insufficiently opposed to the Stamp Act, that he had not taken a strong enough stand against the Stamp Act.

> **They were ready to burn down his house. Everyone advised Deborah to leave. She said, "I'm not doing that." She got a gun. She got some relatives with guns, and they sent away the rowdies who were going to harm the house. Franklin was very pleased, saying, "Well done, Deborah!"**

He still refused to come home. Finally she died. He wrote to a friend that he had to go home, because "my wife, in whose hands I left the care of my affairs, has died." He was not really a nice guy.

EYE: As a journalist, I'll bet you were impressed by these women who had no social media, no computers, who were writing their letters and were very political in their writings.

COKIE: Yes. Diane got intrigued with their handwriting, as well as the content that they wrote. At the very last minute she said to me, "Do you think it would be possible to find all of their signatures?"

So I called around to the various universities, historical societies and libraries where the men's papers are.

Sure enough, we came up with all ten of the women's signatures. What is written under each of their pictures is indeed exactly how they signed their names.

EYE: In terms of what you want to write about, are most of your subjects based in history?

COKIE: Absolutely. My husband is a journalist as well. He writes about living people. I write about dead people. Dead people don't argue with you, which is really nice. I have always been interested in history.

As someone who has covered politics in Congress as long as I have, you spend a lot of time going back and reading what the founders did about various topics like religion in the public square, the right to bear arms, things that come up all the time.

> **I had grown up with political women in a political family and I knew how influential those women were. So I was curious about these women at that very important period in our history. That's how I got started.**

EYE: Do you think we have come a long way in the 250 plus years, in terms of women? Where we are in terms of the political arena?

COKIE: Yes and no. I think the women of the Revolutionary period would be flabbergasted that we have not come further. If you woke them up and told them that women in America did not get the right to vote until 1920, they would say, "No way!" It was already on the table then. It would amaze them. It would equally amaze them that we have not had a woman president.

EYE: Women like yourself were my inspiration to get into broadcasting. Do you think women are well represented now?

COKIE: I think there are now a good many women in broadcasting. A young woman can come into broadcasting and be accepted readily. That wasn't true when I started out.

> **They are moving up and into significant roles. Where you need to see more women is in the boardroom. That is something to change.**

EYE: It's got to be frustrating for you, who follows politics so closely, that there isn't a lot of parity.

COKIE: There certainly isn't parity, but it's a whole lot better than it ever was. Is it good enough? No.

EYE: What do you think about social media?

COKIE: I'm not into it but I think it's fine. Let a thousand flowers bloom. The important thing is not to lose the core values, good reporting, good writing, and communication. Some of the blogging is vituperative and horrible. But there are some very fine journalists out there.

The truth is more people have more access to information than ever before in human history.

EYE: Cokie Roberts, thank you so much. It has been such an honor to speak with you. How exciting to get this new knowledge! We'll keep spreading the word about the special women in *Founding Mothers, Remembering the Ladies*.

First published in March, 2014.

Advice from Our Storytellers

Betsy West and Julie Cohen:
Making documentaries doesn't come simply. Do not try this at home. We came to this with a fair amount of experiences, quite a lot of decades when you put us together as journalists and as filmmakers. I think that helped a lot. Just be persistent and push forward and don't let the little barriers that get in your way get you down.

Jessica Yu:
We are all trying to figure out how to sustain ourselves professionally, but we also have something that roots us and gives us the reason to do it in the first place. Having meaningful stories on one front or another is vital.

Lindsey Seavert:
We need more voices in this industry now more than ever. Follow your passions! Journalists need to bring to light the narratives that are absent and give voice to the voiceless. Also, trust your own instincts, which are far more powerful than you ever realize. Search for light and hope.

Sarah Burns:
Story is everything. Find a story that means something to you and that has resonance. We always find that in looking to the past, we learn something about the present.

Stacey Reiss:
Now that I've been producing for twenty years, I realize that good bosses and mentors don't happen all the time so when you see someone who inspires you, pay attention. I truly love the work that I do. It often doesn't feel like "work." So I think the key to success is finding something you are passionate about.

Heidi Levine:
Go out and follow your heart but be prepared, research the subjects you are interested in covering and try to educate yourself so that you can work as safely as possible. Today, journalists are facing a growing threat so it is critical to educate oneself as much as possible to stay safe and minimize the risks of being targeted.

Karen Shell:
My advice as a photographer starting my own nonprofit to someone interested in founding one is to build strong business practices. Any nonprofit is powerfully founded upon the desire to fill a need and

improve lives. To continue to serve one's mission and grow the impact, the organization needs to be sustainable and adaptable. Promote the organization as you would a business.

Mimo Khair:
I would advise anyone with the passion for photography not to limit themselves to one style or one way of seeing things. Looking at a photography book of one of the masters can enhance your journey more than buying new equipment or obsessing with technical aspects of photography. Always look for more ways to express your story from different angles, different styles until your style reveals itself to you.

Carlotta Gall:
Go to a foreign country, preferably one where you speak the language so you don't have problems with translation. Work for a local newspaper. I went to work for the *Moscow Times* speaking Russian. We were all running around all over the place, just getting these amazing stories. With Twitter, online websites, and blogs, today's youth have even more possibilities. I think in the end the tenets of good journalism are the same. Get the story and get it right.

Dionne Searcey:
I think it's very wise to start with the basics and work your way up for a solid foundation. All the skills we use covering a local city hall or investigating issues and doing the very, very basics of local journalism make it less likely that you'll make as many reporting errors in potentially stressful or unfamiliar situations.

Elaine Weiss:
What I hope is that people read the book, eventually see the film adaptations, and say, "Wow, people fought. People were imprisoned. People suffered. People believed that this nation is a democracy. It is *We the people*, and the greatest gift of a democracy is the ability to vote." How can you be blasé about that?

Fernanda Santos:
Don't be afraid of saying "no." Don't be afraid of asking for help. Don't base your goals and ambitions on the accomplishments of others. Work on being the best version of yourself that you can be.

Zahra Hankir:
If you have a passion or a specific interest, then by all means, chase it, so long as you're committed to upholding the highest journalist standards. As a student at Columbia University, my mentor encouraged me to

write and report the story, and not to shy away from covering my community, people, home country or region, so long as I remained committed to reporting and writing ethically. It was priceless advice that has formed the backbone of my career.

Clarissa Ward:
If you really want to work internationally and particularly in the conflict area, you have to want it so badly because it involves a lot of sacrifice both in terms of your phone going off at 3 AM and missing endless events. It's very stressful and very tiring. It's dangerous so you have to have a passion. If the passion is there, and that is really what you want to do, then don't accept anything else. If you have the fire in your belly, you'll make it happen.

Eleanor Clift:
Honesty makes better copy. It gives it authenticity. It's a lot easier to be honest than to figure out tortured ways of covering up what the truth is. It works and it's much better for your health.

Kim Covington:
Make the change you want to see by developing your own platform, product or channel.

Lee Woodruff:
I can say we are all built to survive. We are resilient. If you are in your dark moments, I promise you will laugh again and touch joy again in your heart. Things are possible! If I can be a role model in that way, then I'm honored.

Laura Munson:
You don't have to do it alone. Find a mentor and a community, and be sure it's a strong match for exactly who you are. I'm hoping people will read *Willa's Grove*, and then say, "You know what I want to do, I want to host a week-long retreat like this." The book begins with an invitation that starts, "You are invited to the rest of your life." I think it's time that we say, "Yes," to the profound invitations of our lives.

Laurie Burrows Grad:
Writing is my outlet. It restored my self and helped me feel more self-worth in concert with more compassion for others. In grief, journaling is most helpful, since you can look back and find your progress and say, "Oh, maybe I do feel better?"

Cokie Roberts:
Get a good liberal arts education, read history and literature, write as much as you can. Work hard!

Book Club Discussion Questions

1. How important is it for people tell their stories?
2. Do you consider yourself a storyteller and what type of stories do you like to tell?
3. Do you have a favorite story that you would like to share?
4. Is there a special talent to storytelling or can anyone do it?
5. Do you like to listen to a story, read one, or view one?
6. Do you have a favorite storyteller, an author, friend, colleague, etc. whose stories you really enjoy?
7. Is there someone in the book whose storytelling has inspired you?
8. Have these storytellers changed the way you look at your life?
9. Why do you think storytelling has become so popular now?
10. Would you be interested in starting a storytelling group where you live or online?

Websites for Updates and More Information

Part I

1. Betsy West, Julie Cohen
   https://www.rbgmovie.com/

2. Jessica Yu
   https://www.jessicayu.net/

3. Lindsey Seavert
   https://www.lovethemfirst.com/

4. Sarah Burns
   https://kenburns.com/staff/sarah-burns/

5. Stacey Reiss
   https://www.staceyreiss.com/

Part II

6. Heidi Levine
   https://heidilevine.photoshelter.com/index

7. Karen Shell
   https://kidsinfocus.org/

8. Mimo Khair
   https://mimokhairphotography.com/

Part III

9. Carlotta Gall
   https://www.nytimes.com/by/carlotta-gall

10. Dionne Searcey
    http://dionnesearcey.com/

11. Elaine Weiss
    https://elaineweiss.com/

12. Fernanda Santos
    https://www.fernandasantos.com/aboutfireline

13. Zahra Hankir
    https://www.zahrahankir.com/

Part IV

14. Clarissa Ward
    https://www.cnn.com/profiles/clarissa-ward-profile

15. Eleanor Clift
    http://www.eleanorclift.com/

16. Kim Covington
    http://covingtonco.com/

17. Lee Woodruff
    https://leewoodruff.com/

Part V

18. Laura Munson
    https://lauramunson.com/

19. Laurie Burrows Grad
    http://lauriegrad.com/

In Memory

20. Cokie Roberts
    https://www.npr.org/people/2101090/cokie-roberts

Photo Permissions

1. Betsy West and Julie Cohen—Storyville Films
2. Jessica Yu—Cover: Braden Moran/Inside: Michael Wawayo
3. Lindsey Seavert—KARE 11
4. Sarah Burns—Courtesy Sarah Burns
5. Stacey Reiss—Courtesy Stacey Reiss
6. Heidi Levine—Cover: Oren Ziv/Inside: Warrick Page
7. Karen Shell—Cover: Claudia Johnstone/Inside: Scott Hayes
8. Mimo Khair—Cover: Andrea Keyrouz/Inside: Shouly Kheir
9. Carlotta Gall—Hiromi Yasui
10. Dionne Searcey—Cover: Rod Searcey/Inside: Tomas Munita
11. Elaine Weiss—Nina Subin
12. Fernanda Santos—Dan Robles

13 Zahra Hankir—Maria Wilson

14 Clarissa Ward—Cover: Kate Brooks/Inside: Scott McWhinnie

15 Eleanor Clift—Courtesy Eleanor Clift

16 Kim Covington—Jenn Isaacs of Any Moment Photography

17 Lee Woodruff—United Way of Westchester and Putnam

18 Laura Munson—Amy Boring

19 Laurie Burrows Grad—Cover: Courtesy Laurie Grad/Inside: Alex Berliner@Berliner Studios/BEI Images

20 Cokie Roberts—ABC News

Books by our Storytellers

Jessica Yu—*Garden of the Lost and Abandoned: The Extraordinary Story of One Ordinary Woman and the Children She Saves*—Houghton Mifflin Harcourt

Sarah Burns—*The Central Park Five: A Chronicle of a City Wilding*—Knopf

Carlotta Gall—*The Wrong Enemy: America in Afghanistan, 2001-2014*—Houghton Mifflin Harcourt

Dionne Searcey—*In Pursuit of Disobedient Women: A Memoir of Love, Rebellion, and Family, Far Away*—Ballantine Books

Elaine Weiss—*The Woman's Hour: The Great Fight to Win the Vote*—Viking

Fernanda Santos—*The Fire Line: The Story of the Granite Mountain Hotshots*—Flatiron Books

Zahra Hankir—*Our Women on the Ground: Essays by Arab Women Reporting from the Arab World*—Penguin Books

Clarissa Ward—*On All Fronts: The Education of a Journalist*—Penguin Press

Lee Woodruff—*Perfectly Imperfect: A Life in Progress*—Random House

Laura Munson—*Willa's Grove: Four Women, One Week, One Question*—Blackstone Publishing

Laurie Burrows Grad—*The Joke's Over, You Can Come Back Now*—CreateSpace Independent Publishing Platform

Cokie Roberts—*Founding Mothers: Remembering the Ladies*—Harper Collins

The Women's Eye Radio/Podcast Hosts

Stacey Gualandi is an Emmy Award-winning journalist with more than 20 years of experience reporting for local, national and newsmagazine outlets, including *Inside Edition, Extra,* Hallmark Channel and KTNV. She has served as host of many entertainment and health & lifestyle programs, and is a contributor to several websites. Stacey is also a certified yoga/spin instructor and was a former Molly Ringwald stand-in.

Catherine Anaya is a three-time Emmy Award-winning journalist, host and media personality. She hosts a YouTube series "Conversations with Catherine" and also serves as a video storyteller, emcee and speaker. She is a former news anchor, recently inducted into the Rocky Mountain Southwest Chapter of the National Academy of Television Arts and Sciences Silver Circle for more than 25 years of broadcast excellence. Catherine is a proud mom of two and a three-time Boston Marathon finisher.

The Editors

Pamela Burke has been a member of the broadcasting industry and print media for more than 30 years as a television executive, bureau chief, producer and reporter. During this time she produced several female-oriented television programs including the award-winning *Working Mother, Attitudes*, and *The Working Women's Survival Hour*. As  the founder of *The Women's Eye* website, radio show and podcasts, she is dedicated to shining the light on people who are making a difference in a positive way and telling their stories.

Patricia Caso was a successful executive producer and producer for 15 years. She then freelanced and did volunteer work for several nonprofits while raising two sons with her husband, Laurence Caso. Having always enjoyed working with people who make an impact, Pat took the oppor-  tunity to combine her producing experience with her regard for impacters to write and interview for *The Women's Eye* in 2012. In 2017, Pat coedited *20 Women Changemakers: Taking Action Around the World* with Pamela Burke.

Twenty remarkable women in our first book will inspire you with their journeys, ideas and advice on how they are making a difference in communities from America to Africa, the Middle East and beyond.

Their journeys are criss-crossed with struggles and triumphs, ideas, hope and ultimately success.

With their strength, fortitude and grit, there are few problems they can't solve, no task they won't take on.

These 20 WOMEN of all ages will give you insight into how change is possible and what it takes to make an impact.

"Those who tell the stories rule the world."

—Hopi proverb

www.ingramcontent.com/pod-product-compliance
Lightning Source LLC
Chambersburg PA
CBHW071807080526
44589CB00012B/715